ate

21B

British
COUNTRY CHEESES

2PK

British

COUNTRY CHEESES

From Devon Garland to Danbydale

◆

PAMELA WESTLAND

WARD LOCK LIMITED · LONDON

Designed by Ann Thompson
Black and white illustrations by
John Spencer
Colour illustrations by
Diana Leadbetter
Text filmset in Century
Schoolbook by
M & R Computerised Typesetting Ltd.,
Grimsby
Printed and bound in Spain by
Cayfosa, Barcelona

British Library Cataloguing in
Publication Data
Westland, Pamela
British country cheeses.
1. British cheeses
I. Title
641.3 '73' 0941

ISBN 0–7063–6678–6

CONTENTS

INTRODUCTION 7

CHAPTER ONE
WHAT IS CHEESE? 11

CHAPTER TWO
A PLACE IN THE HISTORY BOOKS 19

CHAPTER THREE
PERFECT PARTNERS
Cheese and wine 31

CHAPTER FOUR
A LONG TRADITION
The cheeses of the south and south-west 39

CHAPTER FIVE
THE HEART OF THE COUNTRY
The cheeses of the Midlands and East Anglia 59

CHAPTER SIX
SPOILED FOR CHOICE
The cheeses of the north of England 67

CHAPTER SEVEN
A PERSONALITY ALL THEIR OWN
The cheeses of Scotland 75

CHAPTER EIGHT
FROM THE SHEEP AND THE GOATS 83

CHAPTER NINE
CHEESEMAKING AT HOME 91

CHAPTER TEN
COOKING WITH CHEESE 111

SELECTED CHEESEMAKERS 130

INDEX 144

'A poet's hope: to be
like some valley cheese,
local, but prized elsewhere.'

W. H. Auden XII 1958-1971. Shorts II

INTRODUCTION
◆

Herb-covered cream cheeses set out on willow trays for sale at a country market – the Barnstaple Pannier Market in Devon, for one; a log of rich, double-cream cheese rolled in pinhead oatmeal, delicious with Scottish bannocks; a wedge of farmhouse-ripened golden Double Gloucester served with farm cider in a country pub; jars of glistening olive oil packed with discs of peppered goats' milk cheese you can make at home; a half Stilton, creamy and spattered with blue veins, taking pride of place as the port passes round after dinner – there is an exhilarating wealth of traditional and less familiar cheeses being made on farms around the country.

Britain has a proud history and a rich heritage of country cheeses made from the milk of cows – sheep and goats, too – grazed on lush pastures and husbanded in traditional ways. The march of progress – pasteurization on a massive scale, bulk transport and factory production – two world wars (when, in the second, farm production of all but three cheese types was prohibited) and more recently a lack of discernment and discrimination on the part of the public, have taken 'real' cheese to the brink of extinction.

All that has changed, but only in the nick of time. From John O' Groats to Land's End, taste buds are reawakening and farmers, smallholders and artisan cheesemakers (you and me, perhaps) are meeting the growing demand for cheese that is made like cheese used to be made, and tastes like cheese should taste. More and more people who care are turning back the clock, turning up traditional recipes (the Ministry of Agriculture has a fair selection, handed in by regional milk collectors), and discovering the ancient art, or is it craft, of cheesemaking.

In the following chapters we set cheese in its historical context and trace its rise (and in some cases, fall) throughout the regions. The Romans taught us a thing or two about making 'keeping cheeses', and both Samuel Pepys and Shakespeare had their say on the product.

We see how the properties of the soil and the grassland – underlying salt deposits for example – affect the nature of the milk and the flavour of the cheese; what puts the 'blue' into Blue Cheshire, and who has revived Blue Vinney, a noble Dorset cheese that fell by the industrial wayside. We pay an early-morning visit to a Somerset farm to see large-scale, but still traditional, 'cheddaring' and walk two reverent paces behind a cheese grader at work. We drop in on people up and down the country who keep one or two sheep or goats, and get caught up in the infectious enthusiasm for making very, very tasty country cheeses.

We mix and match both traditional British cheeses and some of the newcomers with wines for their mutual enhancement. We shall see just how versatile cheese is in the kitchen (with recipes from soups to salads, snacks to desserts), and see how easy it is to make a wide variety of cheeses at home, in any kitchen, and with no special equipment.

We talk to people in the know, all along the production line, from the farmer through to the merchant and shopkeeper, and on to the discerning customer. Even as their respective problems and complaints are aired – are we being too optimistic? – the gap between what the farmer produces and the consumer wants seems to be narrowing.

Just as the book is going to press, we join in discussions about a claimed scientific breakthrough. Working on the conflict between producers who will not afford longer storage times and the cheese gourmet who resists the blandness of an immature product, research chemists say they have found the answer. They claim to be able to confound even the venerable cheese graders by producing – without using artificial additives – a young cheese which has all the flavour characteristics of one that is well and truly matured.

One's instinct, I have to admit, is to leave well alone – and leave the cheese longer on the storeroom shelf.

Most of all, the book is an appreciation of the real cheeses made today in Britain. Every delicious morsel of them.

CHAPTER ONE
WHAT IS CHEESE?

The aesthetic answer to the question, 'what is cheese?', is that it is a food which delights the eye with its soft, mouth-wateringly creamy texture or its firm, compact, butteriness; that excites the palate with its range of aromas, evoking meadows in springtime and clinking, clanking farmhouse dairies; that pleases the palate with its range of flavours from sweet and mellow to tinglingly, acidly sharp, and resoundingly, memorably assertive; that is as enjoyable on a picnic on a summer's day as it is in the intimate atmosphere of a cosy fireside dinner party; that, in one form or another, can be all foods to all people.

The short answer is that cheese is partly dehydrated, partly solidified, partially preserved milk.

And the scientific answer – well, that takes rather longer and is given in more detail in relation to specific cheeses in following chapters.

Cheese is made by hastening and intensifying the natural souring and curdling process of milk, and then by drying and ripening the curds. Since cheese *is* milk, and is made with recourse to very few additives, the nature of the milk has a profound effect on the nature, and particularly on the flavour, of the cheese. Not surprisingly, the composition of the milk varies according to the species of the animal. It is because the milk of the small dairy animal has a higher proportion of short-chain fatty acids than cows' milk that ewes' and goats' milk cheeses are more pungently aromatic. The composition of the soil, the grassland or other foodstuff and the climate will all affect the flavour of the milk and, equally, the cheese. This is nowhere better exemplified than in Cheshire, where the heavy salt deposits give the regional cheese a unique and inimitable characteristic.

Then there is the quality of the milk to take into account. Some cheeses are made with whole or full-cream milk; some with skimmed; some with a mixture of whole and skimmed milks; some with whole milk enriched with cream and some with a mixture of cows' and ewes' milk or other milk. There is scope here too for a whole variation in the composition and flavour of the cheese because, in dairy terms, fat equals flavour. The fewer the fatty acids present in the milk, the more bland will be the unripened cheese.

Next there is the complex matter of pasteurization. This is a method of heat-treating milk that kills most of the natural bacteria, the microbes in the milk, and enables the milk to be kept 'fresh' for longer – an obvious advantage when it is to be bulk-transported from the farm for mass production in a creamery (the polite word for a dairy-factory) possibly hundreds of miles away.

Pasteurization interferes not only with the subtle, gradually changing flavour of the milk, but with the cheesemaking process as well. It slows down the action of the rennet, which is added to curdle the milk, producing a weaker, slacker curd which takes longer to ripen and develop maximum flavour. Not only that, the heat-treating process, in destroying the enzymes that turn raw milk sour, leaves it short on the ones (the same ones) that gradually ripen the cheese. As to the difference all this makes to the flavour of the cheese, tasting is believing. To work with a professional grader assessing and tasting first a pasteurized cheese and then its non-pasteurized equivalent is opinion forming.

The first stage in the process of cheesemaking is the development of acid in the milk, known as ripening. This can be achieved by leaving the evening's milk to ripen overnight and then adding it to the morning's milk (for centuries farmhouse cheeses were made in this way); by adding soured whey, or by using a commercially prepared cultured starter, which can be selected to introduce the specific characteristics required for a specific type of cheese. The milk is heated to the correct temperature to receive the rennet which may be an animal extract or, resulting in a milder cheese, its vegetable equivalent. Almost immediately it separates into curds and whey. This is the stage at which Little Miss Muffet was consuming her milk solids when her nutritious but, in cheesemaking terms, precipitous snack was so frighteningly interrupted!

With the acidity in the curds developing all the while, the story unfolds in different ways for different cheeses. Fresh, unripened cheeses; soft, white-rind cheeses which are ripened, some with the action of a surface bacteria mould; semi-hard and hard cheeses, pressed and well matured; blue cheeses which acquire the characteristic veining and flavour by the natural or controlled introduction of specific spores. It is a fascinatingly varied account.

FRESH CHEESES

Some fresh cheeses, the kind that make such delicious cheesecakes, enrich pastry, can be used in sandwiches or served with fruit and salads, and are among the easiest to make at home – shades of muslin bags hanging in the kitchen and decorative, heart-shaped moulds draining on a tray. True cream cheese such as the Scottish Caboc (made by draining cream), medium-fat, cream-style cheese (made by draining milk) and yoghurt cheese, all with a soft, granular texture and slightly acid flavour, are not, strictly, cheeses at all, since they are made without rennet. This makes them a delightful choice for someone who has the dairy product and the urge to make them, but is out of stock of rennet.

Curd cheese, or lactic cheese, is another 'nearly cheese', made not with rennet but by the rapid action of lactic acid on the casein (protein) in the curds. They are drained until they reach that soft, spreadable, moist and granular consistency that makes them so good for flans, snacks, grills, toppings and spooning over fruit. In days gone by, curd cheese was made in thrifty households to use up sour, unpasteurized milk, and may be, still, today. Pasteurized milk, however, should be used fresh, and not allowed to sour.

Cottage cheese, also called curd cheese, is a low-fat version, made from skimmed milk. A proud British example is Crowdie, from Scotland (page 77). The American-style cottage cheese, widely available in cartons and made in a small way on some farms, is also acid-coagulated with the curds washed several times to produce the large, irregular, separate particles. Quark, or Quarg, is a sharper, more acidic continental-style cottage cheese, another favourite with slimmers since it too is made from skimmed milk. Usually sold from some farms in shallow cartons, it takes the form of a pure white, thick and slightly granular paste.

Ricotta (we tracked down one Sussex farm-maker in spite of its Mediterranean origins), is a soft, white, crumbly but easily moulded cheese made – and this is the unique feature – from whey, and therefore a by-product of full-fat cheesemaking. The albumen in the whey coagulates on heating (cheesemaking is *always* about coagulation) and gathers up the fatty acids remaining in the however-well-drained whey. The result, a cheese that is perfect with pasta dishes, in Greek savoury pie fillings and with the fruits of summer.

SOFT CHEESES

Think of small, chubby, round or half-round wooden boxes holding highly aromatic cheeses that feel springy to the touch. Think of the kind of cheeses one used to buy only from France – and rejoice. Soft cheeses made on British farms from cows', ewes' and goats' milk are on the up and up.

Coulommier is a word on the tip of many a cheesemaker's tongue these days, and cheeses made in that style are high in the popularity ratings. And that style is. . .? The cheeses are made from soft, renneted curds drained (traditionally) in 12.5-cm/5-in diameter moulds, turned out on to straw mats, rubbed with salt and left for only a couple of days to ripen. The salt dries the surface, a thin white skin forms, the buttery-yellow centre of the cheese softens – and it looks like a cross between Brie and Camembert, which both have a matt, uneven, edible white crust.

The difference is that Brie, which is made in the flat wheel shapes and simulated on British farms, is sprinkled with a bacterial mould, *Penicillium candidum*, and left on straw mats for four weeks, while the mould ripens the cheese. Cheeses made in the Camembert style are sprayed with the mould, dipped in brine and matured for three weeks.

Feta, the Greek-style semi-soft cheese which is proving popular with smallholder cheesemakers and their customers, is made in a different way. The roughly cut curds salted and ripened in their own whey form a moist, crumbly block with no rind.

A 'must' on the cheeseboard, perfect for snacks, and an interesting combination with soft and hard dessert fruits, soft cheeses are unbelievably, meltingly delicious dipped in egg-white batter and deep fried as a starter (page 114). The white-rinded soft cheese – and the Feta type which is so good in salads and pastries – are a versatile addition to the British country cheese scene.

SEMI-HARD AND HARD CHEESES

What a utilitarian, unevocative and distinctly unappetizing way to describe a group of cheeses that embraces such old favourites as creamy, mellow Double Gloucester, crumbly, tangy Lancashire and many new favourites besides! (You will find some surprising and tasty examples in the 'sheep and goats' section.)

Old traditions for making our native cheeses die hard and tribute is paid to them, and more details given, in the coming chapters. It is a long and meticulous process. To take up the story where we left it, the curds are (according to the cheese type) cut, scalded, pitched, piled, milled, salted and packed into moulds. The cheeses are bound or waxed, pressed, matured and graded for quality. And incredibly versatile. Wedges of dairy-golden Cheddar and farmhouse bread for a 'ploughman's'; toasted sandwiches oozing with glistening melted Lancashire; straight-from-the-oven pasta dishes with bubbling cheesy topping; creamy cheese sauces gliding over fish, meat or vegetables; a sizzling fondue pot for a convivial party; whole baby cheeses or sturdy truckles as generous gifts or the perfect act of self-indulgence – 'hard cheese' never had a more appetizing profile.

BLUE-VEINED CHEESES

'Blue' cheeses happen by accident or design. The first Blue Cheshire cheeses, mould-ripened versions of the golden-orange Red Cheshires, were discovered by an accident that proved to be a happy one. Mould had entered the maturing curds and worked its way through the cheese in a network of delicate and, as luck would have it, tasty blue veins. Now this activity is encouraged by providing just the right atmosphere for the cheese to mature and the mould to grow.

Blue Vinney cheese, now being made again from cows' milk in its native Dorset, and several types of ewes' milk cheese are pierced by sterilized stainless steel needles and injected with the mould that puts the blue into that most famous of all sheep's milk cheeses, Roquefort. Stilton, at home in the Vale of Belvoir, is pierced too, to encourage the entry of the penicillium mould ever-present in the air.

So much for the mould the cheesemakers invite into the cheeses, but what of the mould that creeps, unwanted, across the surface of a whole or cut cheese? Don't worry about it. As philosophical and knowledgeable grocers used to say, 'a cheese that attracts no mould is not worth having'. Brush mould off the surface of an uncut cheese and keep it under scrutiny – the spores are not only voracious, they are persistent. Thinly pare affected cut edges, close-wrap the cheese in clingfilm or foil and return it to the refrigerator, confident that no harm will come to it.

In fact, it is rather fun to carry out your own experiment in creating a blue cheese. White cheeses like Wensleydale and red ones such as Leicester and Double Gloucester are prime targets. Leave them, unwrapped, in the company of a piece of blue cheese. If the mould spores take the bait and signs of blueing occur, wrap the 'host' cheese, set it aside for two or three weeks, and earmark a glass or two of port to celebrate its unveiling.

Blue cheeses linger so delightfully on the tongue and are so *made* for good conversation and a congenial atmosphere that many people cannot contemplate them beyond the after-dinner cheeseboard. Which is a pity. In fact, one could go all through a meal with these mould-enriched examples of the cheesemaker's art – Stilton soup; Blue Cheshire gougère with the melting cheese nestling in a puff-ball ring of choux pastry; crisp green salad or avocado with a ewes' milk cheese dressing; blue cheese and egg mousse filled with prawns; poached dessert pears contrasted with a blue cheese sauce. It is good to know you can enjoy these cheeses to the very last crumb.

CHAPTER TWO
A PLACE IN THE HISTORY BOOKS
◆

Legend, always a powerful source of the sublime visual image, and seeking a folk hero, has it that on some remote and inaccessible southern Asian hillside, a wandering nomad milked his flock of sheep – almost certainly the first dairy animals – stirred the thickening milk after a day or so with a faggot of wild herbs and thistles, and lo! The herbs induced mild coagulation, as they would, and cheese was born. The nomad, the legend goes on, continued his wanderings and shared his discovery with anyone and everyone he met. Word got around – and so did cheesemaking.

Archaeological evidence indicates that sheep and goats were domesticated in Eurasia as long ago as 9000 BC and 7500 BC respectively, with cattle coming under the agricultural yoke, so to speak, 1000 years later. The first known portrayal of dairying almost as we know it comes from rock drawings found in the Libyan Sahara desert dating from around 4000 BC, and the most mature piece of cheese yet to be unearthed was found in a clay pot in an Egyptian tomb, circa 2300 BC. Other excavations have revealed sculptures and paintings depicting vessels of every conceivable ingenuity and utility, which can now surely be identified as cheese drainers and moulds.

Cheese was sufficiently well established in Biblical times to have earned a place not only in the diet but in the colloquial language of the day. The bountiful Promised Land was said to be flowing with the prerequisite of cheesemaking, milk and honey. And in the Old Testament, Job in a clear allusion to the creation of form and substance, asks God, 'Hast Thou not poured me out as milk, and curdled me like cheese?'

The ancient Greeks, a society in which the edges of legend and fact tend to become blurred, maintained that cheese was the invention and divine gift of the gods (the demi-god Aristeus, son of Apollo and King of Arcadia, to be precise). They took to it with enthusiasm, appreciating a piece of mature cheese at the end of a meal for one of its supposed attributes especially, its propensity to increase thirst and therefore the diners' capacity to take more wine.

Aristotle, like Job, saw in cheese a deeper, philosophical significance. In his *On the Generation of Animals*, he used the transformation of milk into cheese as an analogy to describe the beginning of human life, comparing the coagulation of milk with the roles of male (the form, and the principle of movement) and the female (the body, or material). 'Here milk,' he wrote of the process of cheesemaking, 'is the body, and the fig-juice or rennet contains the principle which causes it to set.'

Fig-juice as a coagulant features also in a Roman account of cheesemaking, one which gives us both an insight into the variety of coagulants used by the Romans and a step-by-step description of the process. One which has, it is worth noting, changed relatively little in the intervening millenia.

The Romans understood that rennet produced a more advanced kind of fermentation, and enzymes which would continue working and ripening the cheese in store. They used this knowledge to produce hard, mature cheese which nourished and fortified their advancing armies. They even produced enough to work up a flourishing trade in overseas exports.

The Roman cheesemaking technique was simple, yet carried out under sufficiently controlled conditions to be effective. Columella records that once the chosen coagulant was added to the fresh milk, it was kept warm beside an open fire or in the sun. After separation, the whey was pressed out and the curds sprinkled with

salt, both to preserve them and hasten dehydration. The cheese was left out of doors in a warm, shady place to begin the hardening process, then salted once more and dried for a further nine days. Finally, the cheese was washed, dried and packed for storage or shipment. It could almost be a twentieth-century account!

When the Romans advanced on Britain, bringing with them not only their cheeses but their dairy know-how, cheesemaking took on a far more significant role as a valuable means of long-term food preservation. As excavations on sites dating from around 2000 BC show, soft curd cheeses had been made in Britain at least since the Bronze Age. Perforated colanders have been found which could have been used as cheese-wrings or drainers; rush and twig baskets and shallow woven trays were also used. But, useful though they were as a summer seasonal food, these fresh, moist cheeses had poor keeping qualities and did nothing to supplement the meagre winter fare.

Now milk from the huge flocks and herds of milk-producing animals that were kept in Britain at the time, particularly in the highland areas, could be turned to better account. Along with the basic means of producing mature cheeses, the Romans also introduced variety. Some cheeses were steeped in brine to harden them, others coloured and flavoured by being smoked over applewood, and others given a similar, appetizing golden appearance by being coloured with saffron. Hard cheeses were eaten with bread, sliced into salads and included in cooked dishes.

Earlier cheesemaking methods were not entirely superseded, and soft cheeses, some flavoured with herbs or spices, were made extensively in Roman Britain without recourse to either rennet or aromatic plants as coagulants. They were made in rough pottery vessels with spouts, rather like gravy pourers, known as *mortaria*. These vessels had a built-in aid to light coagulation, a gritty inner surface which trapped curd-forming bacteria from one cheese-making batch to the next. The milk was left to set in the *mortaria* and the whey neatly poured off without disturbing the curds.

If not the production of cheese, then certainly the chronicling of it went into decline during the Dark Ages and its true appreciation was probably left in the capable hands of the religious orders. As dairy production, along with all other aspects of civilization, emerged from the dark tunnel of those 'lost' centuries, it is apparent that Britain was subject to an agricultural east-west divide, with cattle the main source of wealth among the Celts in

Wales and the north of England, and sheep among the Anglo Saxons in the east.

In parentheses, it is interesting to note that the duties of a shepherd in the east of England included not only tending and milking his flock, but making the cheese and butter as well. For fifty-one weeks of the year, everything he produced had to be sent to the lord of the manor; but for one week, following the Spring equinox, he was allowed to stock his own larder with all the cheese and butter he could make from the evening's milking. It followed that canny shepherds used every means they knew – salting, brining, drying and smoking – to ensure the keeping quality of their annual perquisites. In Aelfric's *Colloquy*, the salter draws attention to this fact when he reminds the shepherd that, 'You would lose all your butter and cheese, were I not at hand to protect it for you.'

Very gradually, throughout the Middle Ages, cattle began to oust the smaller dairy animals right across the country, perhaps for economic reasons, and increasingly even the peasant's milch animal, his 'commonwealth', was a cow. In the fourteenth century, it was officially recorded that the yield of two cows equated with that of twenty ewes: that is to say a stone (approx 8 kg/14 lb) of cheese, and half a gallon (approx 2 l./4 pt) of butter.

In Medieval times, cheeses were classified not by their geographical location but by their texture – regional variations being considered of little significance – and the three main categories were, quite simply, hard, semi-soft and soft cheeses.

The first type, which by any definition warranted the later derogatory term 'hard cheese', was an inferior produce made of skimmed milk and which, because of its low fat content, set rock hard with long storage. This cheese, unlike the moist and crumbly

examples made in Roman Britain, never found its way to the rich man's table, but was the staple diet of servants, peasants, farm-workers and (because of its almost limitless keeping quality) merchant seamen. Manorial estates unable to produce enough hard cheeses to go round at harvest-time bought in bulk supplies, and thoughtfully provided labourers with enough beer to wash it down. It is safe to assume that the Medieval ploughman's lunch comprised a wedge of this unpalatable hard cheese, a hunk of bread and a mug of ale.

The second category, made from whole or at least only partly-skimmed milk, was a semi-soft cheese of the Brie type which was ripened just long enough to give it a mature flavour and ensure a reasonable shelf-life. This cheese, which had many names, among them Irwene and Rewain, found much favour at high tables, and was used in the preparation of such dishes as sweet and savoury cheese tarts whenever a 'good fat cheese' was called for.

The third category of cheese produced in Medieval Britain, and the one with the longest historical pedigree, was known by the term given to many new, immature foods (wine, too) – 'green'. This fresh, moist curd cheese was sometimes drained, never very thoroughly, on woven mats covered with nettle leaves, and so was also known as nettle cheese.

A much richer curd cheese, a copy of the Normandy Angelot type, was made by combining stroakings with cream from the previous milking. This cheese, which continued to be popular with connoisseurs throughout Tudor and Stuart times, was known as the king of fresh cheeses.

Flavour in fact, has always been a problem with fresh curd cheese, whatever the type of milk used and, following a practice which predates Roman times, country housewives mixed (or 'jumbled') chopped herbs, herb juice or pounded spices with the curds. Sage, marjoram, mint, fennel, walnuts, whatever the additives used, unexciting everyday cheeses were turned into highly individual and tasty 'spermyse'.

Not only tasty cheeses, but colourful ones too and later on, into the eighteenth century, variations of 'spermyse', cheeses were made more for the effect they had on the eye than the palate. It became fashionable to offer a selection of soft curd summer cheeses tinted green with spinach or sage, yellow with marigold petals, red with alkanet and purple with indigo. There were even eye-catching chequerboard designs made by cutting alternate squares from yellow, red, green and purple cheese and so forth.

It was well recognized that cheesemaking was not an exact science, and that there were numerous traps for the unwary, or the careless. Thomas Tusser, a sixteenth-century historian and satirist who was fond of giving his contemporaries' works a new twist of meaning, adapted a poem by Goodman to list what he described as the ten unwanted guests in the English dairy. First the adapted poem, then the explanation line by line:

    'Ghezie, Lot's wife, and Argus his eyes,

    Tom piper, poor cobbler, and Lazarus' thighs:

    Rough Esau, with Maudlin, and Gentiles that scrall,

    With Bishop that burneth, thus know ye them all.'

The first line refers to cheese that was oversalted, white, dry and full of eyes;

cheese that was blown up with its own internal gas, tough and spotted;

cheese that was full of hairs (due to lack of dairy hygiene), or was insufficiently drained and therefore too moist, or full of maggots;

and cheese made from milk that had 'caught' while heating, giving it a burnt flavour impossible to disguise.

Just as the switch to cattle as the main dairy animal made slow progress through the centuries (there are records of huge sharp-flavoured skimmed-ewes' milk cheeses reaching London from south-east Essex in Elizabethan times), so did changes in the dairy techniques.

On the farms, milking, churning and cheesemaking, though physically hard work, were almost exclusively undertaken by women, and in a seventeenth-century account it was noted that 'a

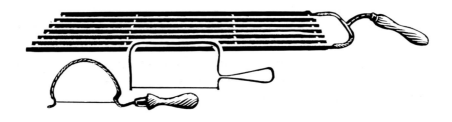

country housewife had to have a cool hand for butter and a strong arm for cheese'. Indeed, the very word 'dairy' lays these tasks squarely in the hands of women. It is a corruption of *dey-ery*, and *dey* in middle English meant a woman servant.

Servants were not always content to eat whatever cheeses came their way. Samuel Pepys' domestic staff complained bitterly about the hard Suffolk cheese they were given, and referred to thin, disagreeable people deprecatingly as 'cheeses'.

Indeed, cheese endures a see-saw of popularity in literary references. Shakespeare does not seem prepared to give cheese his unequivocal blessing. In *The Merry Wives of Windsor* he had Falstaff looking forward to finishing his meal with 'pippins and cheese', yet in *Henry IV, Part 1* he uses cheese in an analogy to signify distaste,

> *'Oh! he's as tedious*
> *As a tired horse, a railing wife;*
> *Worse than a smoky house. I had rather live*
> *With cheese and garlic in a windmill, far*
> *Then feed on cates and have him talk to me*
> *In any summerhouse in Christendom.'*

British cheeses, many of which had long ago shaken off the 'hard cheese' mantle of the Middle Ages, came at last – somewhat belatedly – to be appreciated for their unique local characteristics. By the seventeenth century there were cheese fairs at, for example, Weyhill in Wiltshire, Burford in Oxfordshire, Atherstone-on-Stour in Warwickshire and St. Giles' Hill, Hampshire. Not only that, dairy produce was on sale at other country fairs up and down the land. Cheese merchants did the rounds of these fairs, buying large quantities of fine-quality and lesser cheeses and peddling their wares in other regions and in the towns and cities.

In this way Cheddar cheese, which became established during the seventeenth century, Stilton, and others came to the attention of a wider public.

In the 1690s, an unofficial guild of cheesemongers was formed in London and the national and international cheese market was opened up. Buyers travelled regularly to the cheese-producing regions purchasing almost the entire stock of mature cheeses, which were then sent packing by every available means of transport – road, sea, rail and inland waterway – to be sold from London at greatly enhanced prices. One wholesale syndicate had as many as sixteen ships carrying Cheshire cheese, one of the least expensive of the regional types, from Liverpool to London docks.

Until the middle of the nineteenth century, cheese was made on the farms mainly because the milk was there, and there was usually a surplus. Then two seemingly unrelated innovations brought about the greatest single change to hit cheesemaking since those earliest days on whatever far-away hillside. The French scientist Louis Pasteur discovered the means of heat-treating and purifying milk (page 93), a practice which became commonplace in British dairies by the 1890s. Then the rail network was developed, criss-crossing the country and putting even the most remote farms within a short distance of a pick-up point. Now milk could be quickly transported away from the farms, and making cheese was no longer the do-or-die, waste-not, want-not operation it had always been. Records show that in a period of eighty years at this time the production of Gloucester cheese, for example, fell by as much as seventy-five per cent.

With milk now well and truly on the move, and the Industrial Revolution well under way, the setting up of cheese factories both in the countryside and the towns followed as naturally as one milking session follows another. Derbyshire was in the forefront of this march of progress (if such it may be called) and by 1876 had established five of the first twelve factories to be opened. We take up the threads of each regional story, and see how these and other innovations affected cheese production throughout the country, in following chapters.

Evocative though the by-gone image of the totally rural, straight-from-the-cow-to-the-table method of cheesemaking was, it had to be admitted that without present-day knowledge there were obvious drawbacks, and even dangers. With dairy hygiene a hit and miss affair, if it was considered at all, new milk left in the open to 'work', and storage temperatures and humidity levels difficult to control, it was impossible for anyone in the trade – farmer, factor or merchant – to guarantee quality. Trading or just buying cheeses for the family was very much a case of 'buyer beware'. It has been estimated that as recently as at the turn of the last century, two out of every three cheeses sold proved to be inedible.

Medical men throughout the ages have put cheese under the microscope, and not always pronounced it to be just what the doctor ordered. Alexander Neckham took a very dim view of the cream and curds brought in from the dairy for the lord of the manor to offer guests in the twelfth century. Whether this was because any attention to hygiene in their preparation had been found wanting is not recorded. Such produce, he observed, 'eaten with strawberries or hurts (bilberries), is a rural man's banquet. I have known such banquets hath put men in jeopardy of their lives.'

Hard cheese, the kind that served as the protein staple of the labouring classes, was not particularly well thought of in the medical profession, either. Physicians in the Middle Ages advised their clients to avoid it altogether (advice which may have been superfluous, since by all accounts neither the appearance nor the flavour of such cheeses served to recommend them). It was, however, conceded that a little mature cheese eaten at the end of a meal acted as a digestif, 'to close the stomach'. This view was further expressed in the late sixteenth century when, in a survey of European cheeses, it was noted that Parmesan, 'by age waxing

mellower and softer and more pleasant of taste, digesting whatsoever went before it, yet itself not heavy of digestion'.

Just as the phrase 'hard cheese' lingers in the colloquial language of today as a term of sympathy, so a 'big cheese' denotes someone of importance and social standing – if only in his own opinion. In the eighteenth century, which saw the beginning of co-operative cheesemaking, a big cheese represented a large proportion of the wealth of a community. Villagers who each had one or two cows grazing on common land pooled the milk, carefully noting their share, and a single cheese – bigger in summer, when the yield was higher – was made each morning and evening. Depending on the season, community Cheddar cheeses weighed between 17 and 57 kg/30 and 100 lb.

Big cheeses have long been made to commemorate special occasions, or draw attention to quality. Somerset farmers put Cheddar cheese well and truly on the world stage when they sent a massive five-tonner to the New York State Fair in 1937. And then, in 1976, they paid a collective tribute to the Queen, again in the form of a Cheddar cheese, neatly wrapped in linen and weighing in at 57 kg/100 lb.

Perhaps the most contentious cheese of all time was the one made as a wedding present for Queen Victoria. Here was a thoughtful gesture, a cheese made from a whole day's milking, the production of all 800 cows of East and West Pennard, weighing about half a ton and measuring some 2.8 m/9 ft 4 in in diameter. It was so large that the cheesemakers could think of only one way to press it – between two millstones with an insignia imprinted as a 'follower' (cap).

The young Queen Victoria graciously accepted the gift, but returned it to her loyal subjects for safe keeping, promising to donate £100 to the poor of the parish when the cheese reached a ripe old age – there being a slight suspicion that the cheese as donated might not have been quite mature enough to please the royal palate.

It is to be hoped that everyone concerned realized that it is always the thought that counts. For eventually the cheese, well past its prime and more than a little travel-weary, returned to the farmyard of its origins, where it provided a right-royal meal for the pigs!

CHAPTER THREE

PERFECT PARTNERS
Cheese and Wine
◆

'Cheese and Wine.' The phrase has a ring of familiarity; a sense of harmony; conveys a well-recognized partnership. Cheese and wine do go perfectly together – at least some cheeses go particularly well with some wines. Whether you plan to enjoy a single cheese in all its delicious glory, offer a contrasting selection to demonstrate the wide variety encompassed by the cheesemaker's craft, or are giving a cheese and wine party, there are a few general guidelines that will ensure a perfect match.

Turning the spotlight on each principal British cheese in turn, we start with Cheddar, which is enjoying a flavour come-back. The young, mild, immature cheese is good with young, light red wines such as Bardolino and Lambrusco, and even with some full-bodied whites such as white Burgundies. The more mature the cheese, the more assertive the wine should be. Partner a well-flavoured, mature Cheddar with a medium-bodied red wine such as St. Emilion or Pomerol, or with a sweet white wine, Monbazillac maybe. At the end of a meal, one of the lighter fortified wines such as tawny port or Amontillado sherry would be ideal.

The mellow texture and gentle, smooth, mature flavour of the semi-hard Double Gloucester cheese makes it a good candidate for those occasions when you want to enjoy a particularly good bottle of wine – red preferably. Medium-bodied wines such as Gevray Chambertin and Nuits St. Georges will be well complemented by the cheese. Single Gloucester cheese, with its lower fat content and altogether less luxurious flavour, takes well to any light, red wine.

The slightly salty tang of Caerphilly, the mild, white, semi-hard Welsh cheese with a buttermilk flavour, is at its best with a wine that is on the sweet side of medium. Any red from southern France would be suitable, or a young red Burgundy or a young Rioja.

White Stilton, which has more than a hint of salt and is sold when fairly young, has a strong flavour which is best matched by a rich but not heavy red wine such as one from Portugal or Australia or by a light, slightly sweet wine, Vouvray for example.

The firm-bodied, mild-flavoured Red Leicester, though primarily used as a melting and toasting cheese, is also a good eating cheese. Its clean, fresh taste, reminiscent, as one dairyist puts it, of a spring morning in the country, is enhanced by the Rhône wines, Hermitage for example, and many Italian reds, including Barolo and Brunello.

It is said of Derby, a semi-hard cheese with a natural rind and firm paste, that the flavour blossoms with age, though it is never more than delicately mild. This cheese takes well to red wines of strong character such as Chianti and a wide range of Clarets and Burgundies. Sage Derby, the companion cheese enhanced with the flavour of fresh sage leaves, and especially popular at Christmas, calls for a more powerful choice. The fruity red wines from California, Australia or Sicily, all with the strength of flavour to stand up to the herbs, would go well.

Lightish red wines pay a delightful taste compliment to White Cheshire, the crumbly, slightly salty, creamy-white produce of the north west of England, with Beaujolais, the red Loire wines and Valpolicella all joining the candidates' list. These wines would be suitable, too, to accompany a mild Red Cheshire, but once the cheese becomes more mature it needs a wine with more body such as a red Côtes-du-Rhône or Gigondas.

Lancashire, with its soft, white, crumbly paste, has a wide flavour range. It is often eaten very young when the flavour is mild and calls for a light red wine or a fuller-bodied white such as Rheinriesling. The more mature cheese is better matched to a fuller, more mature red wine, one from Rioja perhaps, or one of the richer-tasting reds from eastern Europe, such as Yugoslav or Bulgarian Cabernet Sauvignon.

The lightly-pressed, slightly-salted, mild, immature cheese of the Yorkshire Dales, Wensleydale is most at home (in wine terms) with any fairly full-bodied white Burgundy such as Macon Blanc or Chablis, or a Gewürztraminer or Pinot Blanc from Alsace.

Blue cheeses need an even more careful choice of wine if the cheese and the wine are to be anything like equal partners in the affair. Full-bodied, well-flavoured red wines, by surprising contrast, sweet white wines, and fortified wines all put up an interesting case.

The traditional partnership of Stilton and port is difficult to fault. According to the occasion and the budget, any port (except an old vintage wine, which is best enjoyed without the benefit of cheese) would be suitable. That puts the choice at anything from an old tawny to a young ruby, or a late-bottled or vintage character wine. Other less conventional options are sweet sherry, Madeira and Sauternes.

These wines are equally good to celebrate the revival of Dorset Blue Vinney; it is worth remembering that the French like to eat their skimmed-milk cheese, Roquefort, with Sauternes or Châteauneuf du Pape. Other good choices to complement the fresh, sharp, 'new' taste of the west country cheese are medium or full-bodied red wines such as Côtes de Beaune Villages, Montrachet and Côtes-du-Rhône.

Blue Cheshire, perhaps the strongest tasting of all British cheeses, needs a strong and preferably sweetish wine to stand up to it. Ruby port or Madeira, the medium-sweet Bual or the sweet Malmsey, are fine choices. As for Blue Wensleydale, the mature and salty north country mould-ripened cheese, red wines of the Corbières or Côtes-du-Rhône types are good – in fact any fortified wine does justice to it – while Sauternes is an excellent choice.

Farmhouse and smallholder cheesemakers in Britain are making some delicious soft-paste cheeses of the Brie and Camembert type, well flavoured and with plenty of 'bite' to them. It is difficult to improve, here, on the natural French partnership of a red, fruity French wine such as Crozes Hermitage, Châteauneuf du Pape or, for a lighter and less costly choice, Fleurie or Fitou.

Some of the most delightful 'artisan' cheeses – made by enthusiastic hobbyists with a feel for the craft – are of the moulded soft curd or Coulommier type. Of these there are many tasty regional examples throughout the book. These cheeses, which have a bland, subtle dairy flavour, are well complemented by a dryish, light red wine or, as a pleasant and summery alternative, a rosé wine such as the light, fruity French country wine Blush, or the more familiar Rose d'Anjou.

These light red and rosé wines go well with the very mildest of the ewes' milk cheeses, which are equally at home, too, with dryish white wines such as Sancerre and White Burgundy. Goats' milk cheeses which have matured long enough to proclaim their origin call for a full-bodied red wine such as the Italian Barbaresco and

Barolo or the Portuguese Dâo. Among the selection from France are Côte Rotie and Côte de Nuits.

Cheeses which have strong 'outside' flavours of herbs, spices and fruits – and there are some splendid examples being made in Britain now – defy the enjoyment of a fine wine. A light, fruity well-chilled white wine complements a cheese with a fresh, herby flavour. Spicy cheeses such as those with peppery overtones are better partnered by medium-dry reds, and the more unusual apricot or lemon-flavoured cheeses make a perfect match with homemade-style country fruit wines or light white wines.

CHEESE AND WINE PARTIES

A fund-raising event for charity; a spur-of-the-moment party when there is no time to cook; a Sunday brunch get-together with neighbours; a teenage or down-from-college celebration; a gourmet's tasting, complete with guidance notes, of British country cheeses and a range of wines. Whatever the occasion, the reason or the excuse, cheese and wine parties are a popular way of entertaining.

When cheese is to be the main course and hold the centre stage, it is usual to allow between 75g and 100g/3 oz and 4 oz per person – the lesser weight for a serious tasting or a money-raising event, with the more generous allowance for an all-evening party or one catering mainly for hungry young people.

Make the selection as exciting as possible, including some of the best-known cheeses (which retain their popularity in any gathering) and some which in your opinion deserve wider recognition. If you have time to plan ahead, talk to your cheese supplier well in advance, to be sure that your selection will be available in peak condition. Take into account the balance of flavours – mild and mature, salty and 'sweet' – and texture, hard, semi-hard, soft and creamy cheese types – and colour, remembering that your cheeseboard will be required to delight the eye before it is tested on the palate. Do take the time to identify each cheese – a little flag with the name and a brief description enhances the enjoyment and spreads the gospel.

If you have stored the cheese in the refrigerator, be sure to take it out at least an hour before the party starts, so that each cheese has a chance to mellow at room temperature and develop its full

flavour. (Some cheeses need more time to 'breathe' – see notes in the following sections.)

Complement the cheeses with a medley of crisp, raw vegetables that are easy to pick up in the fingers, pickled vegetables such as gherkins, shelled nuts and fresh fruits. The season and the budget will have a hand in your choice, but celery, radish, carrot, red and green pepper and cucumber sticks make a varied and colourful selection of crudités, which cleanse the palate and can be used as dip-sticks for cheese dips. Fresh fruits can range from crunchy apples and juicy pears to fresh figs and dates (which are especially good with soft and creamy cheeses), plums and nectarines.

Make your collection of country breads as appetizing as the cheese board itself – French and granary sticks, cottage loaves, wholemeal and white rolls, Scofa bread, black and grey rye bread – delicious especially with smoked and creamy cheeses – potato bread, herb breads, pitta and assorted plain and salted biscuits, all add to the farmhouse feel.

If the party is a gourmet tasting, you might like to offer a small sample of an appropriate and complementary wine with each cheese, allowing time between each serving for discussion and comparison. For a more conventional cheese and wine party, offer a selection of full-flavoured red wines such as those from Burgundy, Bordeaux, Côtes de Rhône and Italy – there are many other suggestions earlier in this section. Among the white wines, you could select from the excellent products of Germany's Rhineland, Yugoslav and Hungarian Rieslings, the white wines of Bordeaux and, for special effect, Barsac or Sauternes, with one or two rosé wines to give a lift to the occasion. An interesting choice here would be Tavel, a dry Rhône wine.

Among the fortified wines, all but the driest sherries are a perfect match for cheese, and cream and brown sherries are a particularly good choice to 'stand up to' blue and other strong-tasting cheeses. Port is an obvious choice too. Ruby port is sweeter and fruitier than tawny, with Madeira perhaps offering the most unusual combination. No Madeira wine is entirely dry, and so none needs be excluded, and they all have a common characteristic – a faint, somewhat burnt after-taste. In ascending order of sweetness, the types are the dry Sercial, Verdelho, Bual and rich Malmsey.

The host at a recent north country fund-raising cheese and wine tasting, having demonstrated the delightful affinity between a medium-sweet Madeira and Blue Cheshire cheese, brought on the pièce de résistance to close the proceedings, underlining that other happy marriage, Malmsey and Madeira cake.

It would be imprudent to conclude a discussion of the enjoyment of cheese and wine without acknowledging that cheese is equally enjoyable with many another sparkling glass. A wedge of Cheshire cheese, that veteran of the English dairy, and a mug of real ale or lager; a slice of Cheddar with a glass of dry cider made on a neighbouring farm; a round or two of pure white goats' milk cheese with a tinglingly cool glass of cloudy apple juice – the combination of whatever cheese and accompanying drink you fancy is a pleasure not to be missed.

CHAPTER FOUR

A LONG TRADITION
The Cheeses of the
South and South-West

◆

To meander slowly through narrow country lanes, see a herd of black and white Friesian cows grazing lazily in the early-morning mist and then to come into the bustling activity of a farm cheese dairy, and later perhaps to enjoy a ploughman's lunch with a glass of cider in a local pub, is to experience the grass roots of British country heritage. To do so in the south and south-west of the land is to turn the spotlight on cheeses that enjoy a world-wide reputation – Cheddar, Double Gloucester, Single Gloucester and Caerphilly – and to discover other, delicious newcomers to the scene that are fast gaining a following.

It was said in the sixteenth century that 'the Cheddar cheese-maker milked whatever milch cow came to his hand, as did his Cheshire colleague; for the secret of his cheese lay in his soil fermentations, not his stock'. With respect to that thoughtful observer, it must also be noted that 'the secret of his cheese' relies very heavily, too, on the way the cheesemaker breaks the curds, judges or measures the acid (pH) content, and controls the storage conditions of the cheese. To watch the anxiety with which a top cheesemaker awaits the pronouncement of the cheese grader – is his farmhouse cheese to be judged fine grade, or sold to the catering trade? – is to realize that the combination of lush pastures and all the care in the world are no guarantee day after day of superb quality.

The true home of Cheddar cheese is in the Mendip hills, the undulating Somerset farmland north of Glastonbury and Shepton Mallet. The parish of Cheddar itself, just one of many surrounding villages where this mature, buttery, hard, tangy and tasty cheese has been made for centuries, was more famous for the remarkable geological characteristics of the Gorge. It is this fact that gave the cheese its name. Visitors flocked from far and wide to see the massive cleft in the rocks, enjoy the hospitality of the inns and the distinctive flavour of the cheese made in the surrounding region (some of it as far away as Dorset, Wiltshire and east Devon) and to take it home with them as 'cheese from Cheddar'. What's in a name? Enough to convince the consensus of local cheesemakers to leave well alone, and let the consumer be the judge.

Cheddar cheese was already gaining distinction and command-ing respect by Elizabethan times, when Thomas Fuller described the cheeses made in Somerset as, 'the best and the biggest in England'. But even then, quality had its price and Fuller went on to bemoan that their worst fault was that they were 'so few and so dear, hardly to be met with, save at some great man's table or rich vintners' cellars'. Throughout the seventeenth and into the eighteenth century, Cheddar cheese was still a luxury, and on the London market could command two or three times the price of the best-quality Cheshire cheese.

If only mass production of Cheddar and other cheeses had been maintained at that local cottage-industry level. Then the super-market shelves today would not be stacked with soapy, insipid examples – the product of the 400 million gallons of milk bulk-carried to cheese factories every year – some of which are a travesty to the proud name of Cheddar.

But the portent is good ('could be better', one impatient cheese gourmet urged me to substitute there). There are now around twenty-four farms in the West Country where Cheddar cheese is still – or is again – being made, proud and true to the old traditions. Armed with a couple of snippets from Victorian cheesemaking accounts, I looked into one or two of these farms to seek reassurance that the craft of Cheddar cheesemaking is safe in their hands.

And the Victorian snippets? One was a document published by a cheese school, set up by the Bath and West of England Society in 1891 to look into every aspect of Cheddar cheesemaking. The scientific research team noted that one herd of cattle showed a marked preference for grazing on one particular field of the school farm, and that herd gave by far the richest milk under review. Conclusion – the ideal diet for a milking herd consisted of ryegrass, dogstail, yellow oatgrass, red and white clover, plantain, daisy and dandelion.

The other nugget of nineteenth-century wisdom was a recipe for Cheddar cheesemaking as practised in the 1850s by a certain Mrs Harding of Marksbury whose cheese commanded a premium price on the markets, and who did her fair share of training young cheesemakers and spreading the gospel of scrupulous attention to hygiene.

In a nutshell – and as taken by Scottish cheesemakers sent south to discover the secrets of Mrs Harding's success – her recipe was: heating the milk; adding whey (the use of a starter was first noted by a Scottish maker later, in 1861); renneting (a standar-dized rennet was not used in the Harding family dairy until 1874); cutting the curd; breaking the curd; first and second scalding; piling the curd; ripening; first and second cutting; grinding, or milling; salting; pressing; binding the cheese and finally storing.

An invitation to visit a large, up-to-the-minute cheese dairy, a converted cider house at West Pennard, in the heart of Cheddar country near Glastonbury contained an element of choice. Would we like to watch the batch of cheese which they would start making at 2 a.m. or the next one, at 7 a.m.? At Newtown Farm, where the Green family keep a Friesian herd, the cheesemaking operation is the highly-organized twentieth-century version of the communal one set up by local cattle holders as a matter of convenience over 250 year ago. The farm is one of nineteen in the west country which makes traditional Cheddar cheese graded and marked by Mendip Foods Ltd., who are the sole agents for farmhouse cheese marketed under the Farmhouse logo.

The milk is brought in from eight neighbouring dairies to be pooled with the farm's own milk production which, under current dairy regulations, is sold to the Milk Marketing Board and bought back at a discount. This is simply a paper transaction – the milk never leaves the home farm – to administer the government subsidy for cows' milk cheese, and known as the cheese rebate.

The milk is pumped directly into a pasteurizer which, to give an idea of the scale of the operation, processes 9,000 l./2,000 gal an hour. It is heated to 82.2°C/180°F and cooled to 28°C/83°F when it is piped into a massive oval 11,350-l./2,500-gal open vat.

Four churns of cheese starter in a tank of warm water are prepared each day for the next. The starter, skimmed milk powder mixed with water and injected with a live culture, is added to the milk in the oval vat and agitated, for even distribution, by paddles suspended on an overhead rail and travelling rhythmically up and down. When the milk is renneted, it immediately changes form and appearance. The paddles, like giant metal fingers, leave trails in the milk as it starts to curdle. Gradually the curds separate and at this stage, still very moist, they are very soft, floating like cotton wool balls in the translucent whey. The paddles, pursuing their there-and-back journey along the tank, create a flurry of turbulence and this must be the closest thing there is to a dairy jaccuzzi.

Steam passes into the cavity wall of the high-sided tank to heat the curds to a temperature of 38°–39°C/103°–106°F according, says cheesemaker David Higdon, to 'how the acidity is going'. A lifetime in the trade enables him to judge this by eye, but he double-checks with a simple laboratory test. The acidity increases steadily throughout the process, from 0.17–0.18 per cent when the milk is

renneted to 0.42–0.43 per cent when, nearly four hours later, the curds are ready for breaking.

But that is a jump or so ahead. The curds and whey travel down a chute and into a deep perforated trough known as the curd table. As the whey is funnelled off into a separator, the drying curd forms a mass, leaving a narrow rivulet of whey running through the centre, like water rippling through sand.

Dave Higdon and his three assistants draw the curds to the side of the tray, pressing out the remaining whey. Small paddles cranked by hand break up the curds and the men draw them up again. They are cut first into two long strips and then into flat cushions which are piled like bricks along the sloping sides of the trough. Then, in a unique process known as cheddaring, they are turned over and over, turn and turn about three times, the last of the whey draining off and the acidity of the curd increasing all the time.

At just the right stage – and this is where the greatest skill in judgement comes in – the blocks are fed into a mill suspended over the trough. Emerging from the mill the small, rubbery lumps of curd are sprinkled with salt and tumbled by paddles to spread it evenly.

Once the curd is broken, it is ready for moulding and pressing. It is packed into cylindrical cheese moulds lined with cheesecloth, covered, and put under pressure for a total of twenty-four hours to compact the curds and expel the air. After two or three hours the ceremony of bathing the cheese is performed, when the cheeses are unmoulded, splashed with hot water and given a change of cloth. The following day the cheeses are tipped out of the moulds again, bandaged – wrapped in purpose-cut cloths dipped in melted lard – returned to the moulds, labelled with the day's date and stored.

Dave Higdon keeps a comprehensive logbook that charts the course of every batch of cheese from the milk carrier to, frequently, the prize-winner's rostrum at county shows. How many gallons of milk were processed – say 1130 l./2500 gal; the type of starter used, whether it was the liquid one described or, occasionally, a commercially prepared powdered type; the time from renneting to milling ('we make our best cheese in 3 hours 50 minutes' Dave Higdon says; how many cheeses were made – there may be fifty-eight, fifty-nine or sixty); the finished weight of each one – it varies between 25.5 and 27kg/56 and 60 lb – all the relevant details are recorded.

After the hustle and bustle of the dairy, the cheese store at Newtown Farm comes as something of a culture shock, and it is not just because the humidity and temperature are controlled. All those cylinders of Cheddar cheese stacked in chronological order on pallets, the rinds darkening with age, are an awe-inspiring sight, especially so when one has just watched the cheesemaking process from A to Z.

The cheeses are stored on the farm for two months and then, if the farm operates under the 'Farmhouse' brand name scheme, they go to the Mendip Foods store in Wells to be graded. This is where they are judged fine, 'catering only', or are sent for reprocessing and eventually, according to their rating, sold to wholesalers and retailers.

Farmers 'borrow back' their cheeses from the cheese store if they want to enter them in shows and competitions, and there is nothing like a row of rosettes around the dairy to make it all seem worthwhile. Dave Higdon demonstrates how a cheese is prepared for judging, stripping off the bandage, scraping off the rind in fine, even shavings and putting a 'showband' around its middle. After about three hours of such individual attention, the cheeses look like fat, rounded cylinders of burnished gold – almost equalling the cheesemaker's understandable glow of pride.

Champion and reserve champion cheeses at the country shows are auctioned at greatly enhanced prices – 'Who'll start me off for this late June fifty-six pounder?' It does any retailer's trade a power of good to be able to offer customers a wedge of a real county show champ long after the showground tents have been dismantled, and the kudos of selling the undisputed best lingers for a remarkably long time.

What is it that makes a cheese a champion, or earns it the

highest marks when the commercial crunch comes? The place to go to find out is the Mendip Foods cheese store in Wells. If the farm store half-a-dozen miles away down the Somerset lanes had something of the air, the serenity and dignity of a chapel, then this one is the cathedral of the cheese trade, with the potential to hold up to 70,000 cheeses in the peak of condition. That means at a constant temperature of 8.8–10°C/48–50°F and a set level of humidity, and aisle after aisle of rack upon rack of greeny-grey-coated cheeses all advancing through the store in chronological order.

The Cheddar cheeses, each one weighing around 25–26kg/56–57 lb, after two months on their home farm, are given their rightful place – at the back of the queue – in the commercial store. Every cheese, handled with the utmost care, is turned head over heels every couple of weeks to ensure an even texture. As the cheese matures, the moisture sinks and the gas rises, and the mould which inevitably and harmlessly forms on the rind is vacuum-brushed off.

Cheeses are graded at two months – the moment of reckoning – in a process more than a little reminiscent of wine tasting. John Plenty, the head grader, accompanied by an assistant and, almost invariably, the farmer/cheesemaker, tests at least two cheeses from every batch. Using an implement rather like an apple corer, he bores diagonally into the cheese from the top and assesses the long golden cylinder of as-yet immature Cheddar with four of the five senses. Aroma; colour and appearance; texture and the *feel* of the cheese; and flavour. The points mount up, and only a cheese which is pronounced fine grade will merit the 'Farmhouse' Cheddar logo. ('Superfine' and 'fine' grades are applied to Mendip Foods grading of Cheshire and Lancashire cheeses at their Whitchurch store in Shropshire.)

After grading, the cheeses continue their progress through the store, maturing all the while, until another moment of reckoning comes. Buyers from the large retail stores and wholesalers come to Wells to taste before they buy, and the boreing – and certainly not boring – ceremony is gone through again. Dave Higdon says that his cheeses are best between six and twelve months, 'but every buyer has his own preference'.

A rare opportunity for a keen amateur the take part in an on-the-spot tasting is too good to be missed. Spotting cheeses made from unpasteurized milk – which mature more quickly – is an art soon acquired, and indeed already possessed by many a cheese gourmet. Sorting out the cheeses from a Friesian herd – over ninety per cent of Cheddar production – from those from mixed herds including Ayrshires and Holsteins, left one languishing at the bottom of the class. And similar and regrettable lack of skill was exercised in sorting out the products of a liquid as against a powdered starter. But, like the cheese buyers who travel to Wells to decide which Cheddars will face us across the cheese counters in the coming months, at any rate I know what I like!

The technique of making Cheddar cheese, its origin so firmly planted in the past, varies little from one farm to the next, and there are a number of west country dairies where one can watch the process at first hand. The Chewton cheese dairy at Chewton Mendip, near Bath, is better equipped than most to welcome visitors, and part of the Waldegrave family estate is given over to leisure amenities. There is a picnic area, a restaurant serving home-cooked lunches, and a caravan park.

Each day 8,000–10,000 l./2,000–2,500 gal of milk from the Friesian and Ayrshire herd is pasteurized and converted into about one ton of cheese, much of it in the usual large sizes, and some in the more homely truckles. These are the neat, chubby little cylinders, in 2-kg, 3-kg and 4-kg/4-lb, 6-lb and 8-lb sizes, that make it possible for cheese lovers to present a whole uncut cheese, perhaps at Christmas time or when giving a party. For these 'small' cheeses, Peppy D'Ouidio, the cheesemaker, uses 100 year old presses, tall, slender frames with a hand wheel, weights and pulleys, that were used in the old farmhouse dairy a century or so ago.

The truckles made at Denhay Farm, near Bridport, and known as Dorset drums are attractively packed as gifts in eight-sided cardboard boxes printed with some of the fascinating history of Cheddar cheese. Ken Corben, the cheesemaker, won four challenge trophies for farmhouse Cheddar at one Royal Bath and West Show,

'using the skills and techniques employed in the Marshwood Vale for generations'. The Denhay cheeses are matured for up to a year to develop the full flavour.

Question. If you are the first person to slice a whole truckle of Cheddar, which way do you cut it? Answer. It is best to cut off the top rind neatly with a sharp knife or a cheese wire and keep it as a lid. Continue cutting the cheese horizontally, taking slices about 2.5-cm/1-in deep and cutting those slices into wedge-shaped portions. The rind around the sides helps to prevent the cheese from drying out, and maintains the flavour for a long time.

Flavour of a different kind is available in the Cheddar cheeses made at Newton St. Cyres, near Exeter on Woodley Farm. There, Cheddar cheese is made every morning of the year – apart from two weeks in August when the milk supply from the Friesian herd is at its lowest – from the morning and evening milk of the previous day. Barry Rowe, the cheesemaker, who says that he trained on a submarine for extreme emotional stability, makes traditional farmhouse Cheddar which is available as mature (nine to twelve months), mellow (six to eight months) and vegetarian mild (three to five months), and two specialities under the farm's Quicke's brand name, herb Cheddar and smoked Cheddar. Double Gloucester and Single Gloucester cheeses are also made on the farm, only recently in quantities which allow them to be 'exported' for distribution beyond Devon.

For the herb Cheddar, chives, thyme, oregano and parsley are added during cheesemaking, to allow the herb flavours to penetrate fully throughout the maturation period. Only the mature Cheddar is used for the smoked cheese, which is smoked on the farm in a traditional smoking oven using oak chips and sawdust. This cheese has a distinctively strong, authentic smoked flavour quite unlike that produced by using smoke-flavoured additives.

It was the Ilchester Cheese Company in Somerset which produced the first speciality cheese some twenty-five years ago by blending Cheddar cheese with beer, a natural combination as any lunch-time beer drinker will testify. Since then the company, now operated on a very large scale and not open to visitors, has gone from strength to strength, and produces a wide and varied range of traditional-style Cheddar cheese with flavour added. To quote but a few: Somerton, the original Ilchester cheese, is a blend of Cheddar with English ale and now also with parsley and a hint of

garlic; Penmill, aptly named, is blended with crushed peppercorns; Albany with cumin seed; Vintage with ruby port; Glenphilly with whisky, and Applewood, no longer smoked over a wood fire, is blended with a filtered smoke extract.

Gloucester Cheeses

The county of Gloucester has been a shire since the tenth century and possibly earlier, and cheesemaking in the region, recorded as early as the eighth century, was important enough to be celebrated by an ancient custom, cheese rolling. The cheeses were conveniently wheel-shaped and had a sufficiently tough outer crust to survive the joyous pastime of rolling and chasing them down the undulating Cotswold pastures. Not only the cheeses, but the custom survives in at least two villages. On Whit Monday, four cheeses are rolled down Cooper's Hill, between Gloucester and Cheltenham, and on Rogation Sunday, three flower-decked cheeses are ceremonially carried into the church at Randwick, near Stroud, to the traditional accompaniment of 'shout, song and music'. The religious part of the ceremony over, the cheeses are taken outside, stripped of their floral garb and rolled three times round the church, 'against the clock'. One of the cheeses is then cut up and divided among the parishioners, and the others are rolled downhill at Wap Fair the following week.

The twin characteristics of a firm, close texture and a thick skin enabled Gloucester cheeses to withstand not only the rough and tumble of festival fun, but a test of quality on the sales floor too. It became the done thing for prospective buyers to jump up and down on the cheeses to assess their grade and by this means, markedly less subtle than grading by boreing, eliminate any that were

loosely moulded, had a thin crust or contained too much gas (for which the derogatory term was 'hoven').

It was not these qualities of unusual durability, however, that first – at the end of the sixteenth century – brought Gloucester cheeses to the notice of buyers from beyond the regional boundaries of the Vale of Gloucester, the Vale of Berkeley and the Cotswolds. It was the rich creaminess of the flavour, attributable to the combination of lush pastures and, more particularly, the county's own native dairy cattle, the Gloucesters. This hefty black, chestnut and white ancient breed, which has been likened in appearance to wild oxen, gave a particularly rich milk yield, its high fat content contained – ideal for cheesemaking – in small globules. It is practically impossible to find a cheesemaker of Gloucester who does not sooner or later refer to them as 'this noble breed'. For 150 years, the Gloucesters – both cattle and cheeses – went from strength to strength until, in the mid-eighteenth century, disease struck the herd, and Longhorns and Shorthorns were brought in to reinforce them. Within fifty years, the old Gloucesters were a dying breed, a fact mourned by William Marshall who in 1796 wrote, 'For dairy cows, I have not, in my own judgement, seen a better form . . . it was the Gloucestershire breed which raised the Gloucestershire dairy to its greatest height.'

Happily, the use of the past tense when referring to the breed is no longer appropriate, since in the last two decades strenuous efforts have been made (page 53) to revive them.

Cheese academics agree to differ on the origin of the classification of Single Gloucester and Double Gloucester cheeses, while gourmets rate both cheeses highly, when they are made on the farm by the traditional method. Both cheeses are 39cm/15½ inches in diameter and shaped like a millstone, the 'single' cheese at 6cm/2½ in being traditionally roughly half the depth (10.5cm/4¼ in) of the 'double'. This difference alone is enough to satisfy some people as to the origin of the descriptive terms.

But that is not the whole story. The Single Gloucester cheese was originally made from the skimmed milk of the evening's milking, left overnight to ripen, and then added to the whole morning's milk. Thus it had a single complement of fat and solids, a lower acidity and was made at a lower temperature.

Such cheeses, which were made almost exclusively during the spring, from the early season's milk, matured more quickly and were ready for eating within two months. This was in good time to fortify the labourers working in the hayfields, and thus they came to be known as 'haymaking cheeses'.

Double Gloucesters were made from the whole milk of the morning's milking alone or, depending on the time of year, with the whole of the previous evening's milk, or the cream skimmed from it. In any event, they had a higher cream/fat/acid content than 'singles'. The longer maturation period of Double Gloucester cheeses would naturally have resulted in a deeper colour, but this was always intensified by the addition of beetroot or carrot juice to the milk. The distinctive warm, rich, golden colour still survives as a characteristic and is now achieved by the addition of annatto, a dye obtained from a tropical tree.

This inner hue, not being apparent until the cheese was cut, was not enough to satisfy merchants in the eighteenth century, who decided that they should proclaim the excellence of their wares in a more perceptible way. They therefore daubed the rinds with gaudy red dye and paint, and it was in this eye-catching garb that Double Gloucester cheeses were carried by barge from Lechlade down to London, where in 1783 they sold on the wholesale market at 3¾d per pound. Others had a shorter journey and were sold at the cheese fairs at Lechlade, Berkeley, Stow-on-the-Wold and the Barton Fair at Gloucester.

The conditions under which cheese is stored and matured have always been of the utmost importance, and made a significant contribution to the character and quality of the product. Some of the considerable output of Cheddar cheese was stored in the effectively chilly atmosphere of the Cheddar caves; Roquefort, the remarkable French ewes' milk blue cheese, is matured in the limestone caves at Columbou, and there are many other such examples. Single and Double Gloucester cheeses traditionally had more homely quarters, in the purpose-built attic rooms high at the top of the Cotswold stone farmhouses. Many sixteenth and seventeenth century examples of such houses still exist, their cheese rooms extending from gabled end to gabled end and recognizable at a glance by their tall, narrow ventilated but unglazed windows.

The way Single and Double Gloucester cheeses were made in the cool, cool, cool of the dairy with its stone floor on the north side of the farmhouse, differs in detail but not in general principle from Cheddar making. The milk and the skimmed milk or cream (according to type) was warmed to a temperature of 29°C/85°F or

slightly higher in the depth of winter. The colouring and rennet added, the curd set in anything from 40 minutes to 1½ hours and was cut into small cubes with a triple cheese-knife. The whey was drained off, the curd gathered into a mass and then cut again. The whey was heated, poured over the cut curds, stirred vigorously to heat them (the traditional method of doing so) and drained again. The curds were then packed by hand into moulds, the excess whey being squeezed out in the process – oozing in trickles through experienced fingers working rapidly to pack the wooden moulds. These were covered, stood at an angle to drain off any remaining whey and then weighted. After a couple of changes of cheesecloth, and when they were compacted and diminished in volume, the cheeses were turned out of the moulds, disrobed, and rubbed generously with coarse salt – using 'as much hanging to it as would stick' – which would dry the outer surface of the cheeses and start the formation of the crust. Returned to the moulds and turned daily, the cheeses came under increasing pressure, until they were unmoulded, left in the dairy for ten days and then bathed in whey.

Next came the beauty treatment, when the cheeses were scraped with a blunt knife until the surface was smooth and shiny and bore no tell-tale traces of the criss-cross weave of the cheesecloth. A good finish was a profitable sales aid, and some cheesemakers went to extra lengths to achieve it – and a higher price at market – polishing the cheeses with a small bristle brush like a shaving brush, working in circular movements until the surface glowed like burnished gold. The final touch was a coat of rich whey butter rubbed in with a cloth, to give what one factor described as 'a fine saleable yellow'; and what must surely have appeared more appetizing than the daubs of red paint.

It was now time to carry the cheeses to the drying atmosphere of the cheeseroom up aloft where, after four or five weeks, they were stacked two or four high. By then the crust had developed enough for them to be not only stacked, but thrown about like old cheeses, as William Marshall put it. And a few weeks later they would be equal to the task of being rolled down hill, or jumped on by a suspicious buyer.

The romance and labour intensiveness of the traditional way of making the cheeses was no match for the Industrial Revolution, and factory production began in Gloucestershire in 1875. So profitable was this new speeded-up process that the large and rapidly-growing-larger creameries employed agents to go round the farms and farm equipment sales to buy and, tragically, destroy the cheese vats, the curd cutters and agitators, the knives and strainers, the cheese presses and troughs that had been used in the dairies for generations.

A few, however, escaped their grasp and cheesemaking continued sporadically, and even diversified on a few farms. At the turn of the century a Dr Bond produced the Little Gloucester, a small thin-rinded, block-shaped cheese, and the Gloucester Roundel, a perfect sphere which could be eaten immature, when it was sweet and mild, or left to ripen and develop full flavour. One thing it was neither designed nor recommended for, though, was bowling downhill!

Factory production of the cheeses eventually succeeded in blurring the regional boundaries, and now Double Gloucester cheese is made on a large scale in creameries as far apart as the south coast and Lancashire. Comparatively small quantities are also made on farms under the Mendip Foods 'Farmhouse' quality label, some of which is made in the traditional millstone or wheel shape, and there are a few farms where it is made in domestic quantities.

For the true pride in the time-honoured old Gloucester breed and the cheeses, the story switches to Dymock in Gloucestershire – where else? – where at Laurel Farm Charles Martell is very busy fulfilling his life's ambition, to revive the herd. By 1974 it was in danger of extinction, with only forty-five head surviving. Approaches to all the buyers at the last dispersal sale located the cattle, scattered throughout the country in ones and twos, and enabled Charles Martell and his wife Monica to re-form the Gloucester Cattle Society. Within five years there were 100 head, and gradually the Dymock herd is being built up. And cheeses, real Gloucester cheeses made with unpasteurized milk from Old Gloucester cows, are now being made on the farm. Charles Martell makes Single Gloucester cheeses in traditional 4-kg/8-lb wheels or small cylinders with natural unpainted crusts – no red dye – and sometimes with herbs or nettles; Double Gloucester cheeses, usually without added colouring, in wheels of various weights, and, a close cousin, Double Berkeley in 4-kg/8-lb wheels. As for distribution and availability, it is growing all the time. If you want to taste Charles Martell's cheese, he says, just shout! More specifically, he sells it at Cirencester, Gloucester and Ledbury markets (see below).

If the tale of the cheeses of Gloucester is generally one of diminishing quality coupled with increasing production, the story of Dorset Blue Vinney comes close to tragedy. The name derives from the old English word for mould, vinew, and the cheese derived from the milk of Old Gloucester cattle over-summering in rented pastures in Dorset. In the seventeenth century Blue Vinney was held to be the best, indeed the only good, skimmed-milk cheese. It was pressed from sour skimmed milk collected from several days' milkings, producing a very acid curd which soon 'made', and set very hard. The best of all cheeses were said to be made from the milk of a single cow, and so Buttercup, Daisy and Chestnut would each have had their own section of the dairy shelves.

The thin crusts of the low-fat cheeses gave easy access to the mould spores present in the damp dairy conditions, and the cheeses were quickly blued by veins of the mould ripening from within. But many cheesemakers left nothing to chance and resorted to such practices as stirring the milk in the vat with a mouldy harness or leaving a pair of boots of questionable cleanliness alongside the milk so that the lively spores were but a short hop, skip and a jump away.

Blue Vinney cheese had its imitators, notably Stilton cheese of inferior quality and Cheddar cheese which had inadvertently been subject to mould development. It had its detracting influences, too, notably the introduction of machines which automatically and, for this purpose, much too comprehensively skimmed the milk. The cheeses made with the resulting fat-starved buttermilk bore little resemblance to the original knife-resisting Blue Vinney.

Farmhouse cheesemaking nationwide, and Dorset Blue Vinney in particular, suffered a terrible blow during World War II. The Ministry of Food proclaimed that only long-lasting, mature Cheddars, Cheshires and Wensleydales were making a suitable contribution to the nation's war effort and even the naturally hard, mature Blue Vinney was axed. Milk from the farms was bulk-carried to the factories which took over cheese production. After the war, it was the fully-automated factories which continued to produce by far the bulk of the nation's cheese requirements – though not Blue Vinney. Many farms, in Dorset and elsewhere, never again picked up the threads of centuries of tradition.

But recently, within the past five years, one farmer has done just that. Mike Davies, who confidently describes himself as 'the only maker of Dorset Blue Vinney cheese in Britain' has set up his dairy for production of the old cheese in the traditional way. He acquired several of the old recipes which had been left at the Ministry of Agriculture by various milk officers and, as he says, 'jiggled about with them' until he found one that would fit in with his farming methods and produce a cheese that was reasonably easy to control.

Mr Davies makes his Blue Vinney from the whole morning's milk of his Friesian herd with some skimmed milk added. This produces a cheese with between 3.0 and 3.3 per cent fat content, slightly higher than the original cheese made with hand-skimmed milk. The introduction and growth of the penicillium mould varies with the season and conditions, and Mike Davies spikes some cheeses – using stainless steel needles – to encourage spore development.

The Dorset cheeses are made in two sizes, 6.5kg–7.25kg/14 lb–16 lb, which are matured for between three and five months and, especially at Christmas time, small truckles weighing 1.5kg–2.25kg/3½ lb–5 lb which are matured for two months, both simply wrapped in paper covering.

The consistency of the cheeses varies from month to month – 'the cows are on different rations at different times of the year, and it shows in the cheese'. Blue Vinney has something of the appearance of a Stilton, a light creamy-coloured paste closely mottled with darkish blue veins fairly evenly distributed through the cheese. And as to the flavour, that is not like Stilton at all, milder yet slightly fresher and sharper.

From a cheese with a long pedigree we move on to a new range developed by a cheesemaker in Reading – proof that British cheeses do not rest on the laurels of tradition. Mrs Anne Wigmore trained in cheesemaking at the National Institute of Research and Development at Shinfield in Berkshire where in a total of ten years

she spent five years on cheese flavours and research into different cheeses. Besides Spenwood, a ewes' milk cheese, she makes soft fresh Coulommier-type cheese from Friesian cows' milk with garlic and herbs, or chives in 250-g/8-oz rounds, and 100-g/4-oz pots of lactic curd cheese with the same flavours.

Under the Village Maid brand name of the Spencers Wood dairy on the edge of the Duke of Wellington's estate in Reading, Anne Wigmore makes an unpasteurized matured cheese from the Guernsey herd, called Wellington Golden Guernsey. It is made in small, flat cylindrical cloth-lined moulds stacked one above the other and pressed. It is then matured in the cellars of Stratfield Saye House. This full-fat, hard cheese has a delicately sweet flavour and fruity aroma.

Southwards to Devon, half way between Exmoor in the north and Dartmoor in the south, we come to Tony and Ann Dickman's farm at Winkleigh. Here their Friesian herd benefits from the superb grazing conditions which Ann Dickman, the cheesemaker of the family points out, include abundant rain. The farm is moving towards becoming organic, as the Dickmans use no pesticides, make only limited use of fertilizers, and use no routine chemicals or antibiotics in the dairy.

And now for the cheeses. Wheatland is an unpasteurized, full-fat soft cheese with a bloomy white crust, made in 250-g/8-oz rounds. It can be eaten young at fourteen to twenty-one days old or ripened to twenty-eight to forty days, when it has a creamy curd and strong flavour. This cheese resembles French farm-produced cheese and is totally unlike pasteurized factory-produced cheese. Wheatland Moor is a semi-hard cheese with either a natural or washed rind in 1-kg, 2-kg and 3-kg/1½-lb, 3-lb and 5-lb rounds. It has a good flavour which improves with keeping, and is not sold until it is two months old.

Say Wales, and then cheese, and the natural word progression is Caerphilly, the smooth, white, semi-hard cheese which originated – but is now no longer made – in Glamorgan. The original farm cheese with its close, flaky texture was slow ripening and had a mild flavour with subtle salty and acidic overtones. It was much appreciated by miners because it remained moist for long periods when they took it underground in their dinner-bags.

A version of the cheese, with a much higher salt content, is made in creameries in Dyfed and Powys and is said, by those able to make the comparison, to be whiter and more acidic than the original.

Say Wales, and then farmhouse cheese, and people in the know will now say Llangloffan, which is the name of a small hamlet close to the spectacular Pembrokeshire coastline and consisting of little more than a cluster of farm buildings. This is where Leon and Joan Downey, who describe themselves as city folk, settled from Cheshire in 1977. Leon Downey was a viola player with the Hallé Orchestra and his wife a secretary when they decided to face the challenge of making a living from a run-down, allegedly non-viable fifteen-acre smallholding.

What they brought with them, apart from their unbounded enthusiasm for 'real cheese' and an admitted lack of agricultural experience, was an understanding of the kind of food they and other people were beginning to demand. Their ambition, now already gratifyingly fulfilled, was to build an enterprise which produced high-quality, uncontaminated food and at the same time involved the public. They set out to strike a balance between a total commitment to natural organic farming methods, building a fine dairy herd – they settled for Jerseys – making traditional cheese and welcoming visitors. Quite a juggling act! Now posters advertising the farm as 'the cheese centre of Wales' invite people to 'stroke a Jersey cow, relax over coffee or just stroll around the farm'. The Downeys make full use of animal waste and calcified seaweed spread on the land in the winter, and nature, they say, does the rest. The farm has been awarded the Soil Association Symbol of Organic Quality whose standards cover the management of the grassland and the cows.

The fawn, or cream-coloured cows, produce about 2,750–4,500 l./600–1,000 gal of milk each lactation and are milked by machine. The milk is cooled – the Downeys do not practise pasteurization – the starter added and then, 1–1½ hours later, renneted. The most delicate part of this cheesemaking operation is cutting the curd which is done with vertical and horizontal knives very slowly and carefully to prevent the fat escaping from the curd particles. When the particles are small enough, they are stirred by hand in the old traditional way and at the same time cooked by heated water in the jacket of the cheese vat. Once the whey is drained off – it goes to feed the pigs, calves and cows – the curd is cut into blocks, turned every 10 minutes and piled. After about 50 minutes the dry, acid curd is ready for milling, then the salt, chives and garlic are added. The curds are piled into the original wooden moulds from the farm, lined with cheesecloth, pressed slowly at first, turned in the moulds and pressed until the curd is eventually transformed into a closely-knit cheese.

The cheeses are unmoulded and left to ripen on wooden shelves from six weeks to twelve months, depending on the texture and flavour required. However long the cheese is matured, that flavour is gentle and refreshing and never bites back at you.

Llangloffan full-fat hard cheese, with a natural crust, is made in 1.5-kg, 4.5-kg, 10-kg and 15-kg/3-lb, 9-lb, 20-lb and 30-lb cylinders. Red Llangloffan with chives and garlic is available in 1.5-kg and 4.5-kg/3-lb and 9-lb sizes. Both are available from the farm, where visitors may watch them being made. The farm was awarded HRH The Prince of Wales' Award in 1986.

Another new organic, unpasteurized cheese from west Wales, Pencarreg, is made by Welsh Organic Foods in Lampeter with milk from four family farms in Cardiganshire. Here, too, the farming practices are aimed at building the biological fertility of the land, a fact – recognized by the Soil Association Symbol of Organic Quality Award – which gives the cheese a distinctive quality.

Pencarreg is a full-fat soft cheese with a smooth, creamy texture. Initially it has a delicate flavour that develops when the cheese is kept, bringing out the individual character that would not be perceptible, or indeed present, with the use of pasteurized milk.

The cheesemaking process has been undergoing extensive trials at the Caldey Islands Dairy on the island off Tenby, in Dyfed, where Dave Philippart, who qualified at the Cheshire College of Agriculture, runs a Jersey herd. The trials were successful and now production is under way. The location of the cheesemaker's City & Guilds' training may in some measure account for the type of cheese being made – an unpasteurized Cheshire type with a natural crust. The cheese, and a wide range of cheesecakes is available locally, at the island's tea garden shop.

The importance of cheese as a domestic commodity in Medieval Wales is evident from what we read in an early Welsh divorce law. Lawyers and their clients must have worked together to calculate the ideal time for a marriage break, according to the season and the progress of the cheese through the dairy:

'To the wife belong the meat in the brine, and the
cheese in the brine; and after they are hung they
belong to the husband; to the wife belong the vessels
of butter in cut, the meat in cut and the cheese
in cut.'

CHAPTER FIVE

THE HEART OF THE COUNTRY
*The Cheeses of the Midlands
and East Anglia*

◆

The brooks and valleys of Leicestershire, Derbyshire and Nottinghamshire offer some of the richest, most undulating pastureland in the country; some of the best fox-hunting too. The concept that contented cows grazing nutritious meadows equal the finest cheeses is nowhere more evident, with Blue Stilton cheese the most renowned and creamiest of all.

The first records of the cheese appear to date from the early eighteenth century when it was made by a Mrs Paulet, a farmer's wife living near Melton Mowbray, whose brother-in-law, Cowper Thornhill, kept the Bell Inn at the village of Stilton, over the county border in Huntingdonshire (now Cambridgeshire). The coaching house, on the Great North Road, was well placed for passing trade and the family cheese was served to travellers stopping over en route between London, York and Edinburgh. It was not long before news of this mild, rich, blue-veined 'cheese from Stilton' had spread beyond the arterial road and throughout the country, and its reputation as king of the English cheeses became well established. At that time, the canny landlord was able to sell the cheese for the then princely sum of 2s 6d per pound, though its price in the markets was considerably lower.

For a time, the recipe for the cheese remained a mother-and-daughter monopoly, its secret not fully understood by outsiders. By the end of the eighteenth century the family recipe, or one very like it, had spread through most of the small dairies in the surrounding vales, and one village, Dalby, even paid its annual tythes in the cheese. Factory production came to the dales in 1870 and individual versions of Blue Stilton, still retaining the original characteristics, were made on a large scale.

It is easy to see – from the way the production of other cheeses developed – that Stilton making could have got out of hand and spread far beyond its traditional homeland, with consequent loss of identity. Indeed, for a long time it did, and in 1910, realizing the dangers, the principal makers grouped together to protect their boundaries. They defined the territory where the cheese could be made as the Vale of Belvoir, which links the southern borders of Derbyshire and Nottinghamshire with that part of Leicestershire (now including Rutland) north and east of Melton Mowbray. They defined the character of the cheese, too, and this was when its production 'passed from the stage of a secret recipe guarded by farmhouse makers to become an ascertainable process'. This declaration was given the protection of law in 1969, since when it has become illegal to describe any cheese as Stilton that is not made in the traditional way in the Vale of Belvoir.

And what is the nature of this cheese that has merited such protection? In the High Court judgement, Stilton was defined as, 'a blue or white cheese made from full-cream milk with no applied pressure, forming its own crust or coat and made in cylindrical form, the milk coming from English dairy herds in the district of Melton Mowbray and surrounding areas . . .'. But, with respect to their lordships, that is to over-simplify the case. Early records show that one important factor was the number of separate curds used – it might be three or two – and another of course was the way and the stage at which the mould spores were introduced.

Some of the early Stilton makers, perhaps in an effort to outshine their neighbours, made their cheese extra rich by adding the cream of the evening's milk to the whole morning's milk (in the way of some Double Gloucester recipes). Others bathed the curds in wine to encourage bacterial growth, and some poured wine or beer over the ripening cheeses.

It takes 77 l./17 gal of the milk to make one cheese or, put in more domestic terms, just over 4.5 l./1 gal of milk to make 500g/1 lb of Stilton. The milk is pumped into stainless steel vats, where a starter culture and rennet are added and stirred into the milk, usually by hand. Curds form from the milk solids and after an hour or so are cut first with horizontal and then with vertical knives to help release the whey. The following morning the curd is cut into 15-cm/6-in blocks, milled into walnut-sized pieces and salted, then tipped into cylindrical 'cheese hoops' or moulds, each one standing on a draining board. The cheeses are left at a temperature of 21°–23°C/70°–74°F in what some dairies call a 'hastening room' for seven days, and turned daily by hand to ensure an even distribution of moisture.

By then the curds will have settled and the cheeses are removed from the moulds and smoothed and scraped with special knives to prepare the surface for the formation of the coat, or rind. This process also prevents oxygen from entering the tiny air pockets still existing between the lumps of curd. At some dairies, the cheeses are wrapped in clean muslin and returned to the hoops for a further two days.

The young Stiltons progress through the dairy in rooms known variously as the white room, maturing room and coating room, where they are turned daily at first and then on alternate days, at

carefully controlled temperatures between 12°C/54°F and 15°C/60°F.

When they are six weeks old, the cheeses are pierced with stainless steel needles about the size of skewers, to allow air to penetrate to the heart of the cheese. This activates the penicillium mould present in the curd, and very shortly the characteristic blue veining begins to appear. The cheeses are then left to ripen for seven days, during which they are turned on every third day, and then they are pierced, or skewered again.

Towards the end of the ripening period, at about the eighth week, a cheese grader 'irons the cheese', that is to say checks the quality by inserting a grading iron diagonally from both the top and bottom of the cheese. The pencil-thin sections of cheese drawn out by this apple-corer-like instrument present a cross-section of the inside of the cheese, enabling it to be assessed and graded according to the extent of ripeness and the openness of the texture. This varies not in relation to the age of the cheese but from one maker to the next, and is largely determined by the firmness or otherwise with which the curds are packed in the hoop. Trade buyers can select the degree of ripeness their customers prefer, and have the cheeses packed and despatched accordingly. The cheeses are usually sold at between two and three months old.

Good Stilton is creamy-white or deep cream in colour, with the blue veining, which makes it more 'live' than any other cheese, evenly distributed and radiating from the centre. Unlike pressed cheeses which harden with age, Stilton becomes creamier and more crumbly – which is probably why in Victorian and Edwardian times a 'ripe old Stilton' was served with a long-handled cheese scoop. In this way the centre was spooned out, leaving the coat intact, protecting a rim of hardening and virtually unattainable cheese. (Some experts estimate that over half the weight of a cheese could be wasted in this way.) Stilton makers consider this, and the other remnant of a by-gone age, that of pouring port into the centre of a cheese, a travesty. 'That way,' says one maker firmly, 'you ruin two products in one operation.'

You can buy Stilton gift-wrapped in pottery jars, in wedge-shaped packs, in whole or half cheese of various sizes, and of course cut to your requirements. The cheese can be frozen successfully, and should otherwise be stored at a constant temperature between 5°C and 10°C/40°F and 50°F, which is the temperature of the main compartment of a refrigerator. It should be wrapped in clingfilm or put in a lidded container to prevent it both losing moisture and picking up other food odours. To restore the full flavour of the cheese after cool storing it should, ideally, be loosened from its wrappings and brought to room temperature for several hours – which means thinking ahead.

If you have a whole (7.25–7.5kg/16–17 lb) or half cheese, for a party or at Christmas time when Stilton, walnuts and port are the traditional combination, it is best to keep it in a cool place (not above 10°C/50°F) covered with a cloth dampened with brine.

White Stilton is a different type of cheese, delicious in its own right, and stands comparison with other milky-white cheeses, but not with its older brother. White Stilton is the moist young cheese, sold after four weeks' maturing, before the blue veining begins to develop. It has an open, crumbly texture (because it is not pressed) and a fresh, refreshing, mild flavour.

The smallest Blue Stilton dairy of the nine is Webster's, in Saxelby, Leicestershire, which was set up in converted farm cottages and is where the old-fashioned, labour-intensive ways of making the cheese are still used. Mr M Fropwell, the cheesemaker, trained at the dairy and also at the Nottinghamshire School of Agriculture, and is a member of the Society of Dairy Technology. He produces eighty creamy, mature, pasteurized Blue Stiltons a day, and White Stilton which, because of its resemblance to Lancashire and Wensleydale cheeses, is popular in the north of England.

There is an obvious territorial overlap in Stilton country, and some dairies in the heart of the Leicester cheesemaking region produce both cheeses. One such is the Tuxford & Tebbutt dairy in Melton Mowbray, which once had close links with the pork pie trade and is now owned by Express Dairies. The bulk of the creamery's Leicester output is in rindless block cheese destined to be vacuum-packed for the supermarket shelves.

Red Leicester, a distinctive, rich, russet-coloured cheese is made in the traditional wheel or millstone shape. With these two characteristics in common with Double Gloucester, it is probable that Red Leicester, which has been made in the county at least since the late sixteenth-century, is an immigrant which found its way northwards through the Midlands from Gloucestershire.

For a time, earlier this century, the use of a colourant in the cheese was prohibited by law, it being felt that its use concealed any deficiencies in quality, and so White Leicester was produced.

The cheese has now been allowed to revert to its former glory, the colour coming from the use of annatto, which is found in the seed pods of a tropical tree. This is the only permitted cheese colourant, and the one which gives Double Gloucester its similar, though lighter hue.

Red Leicester has a higher moisture content than Cheddar (and is therefore softer), and matures within two or three months to produce flaky, semi-hard cheese. It has a clean, fresh taste with the flavour of the full-cream milk clearly discernible. Many people prefer the cheese when it has been matured for six or even nine months, when it becomes dry and develops an almost nutty flavour. The cheese coat naturally develops a blue mould in the process of maturing, and the growth is encouraged in the cheese store by leaving the whole cheese unwrapped.

Sadly, Red Leicester is the sole survivor of a range of local cheeses that were once made in these 'shire' counties.

However, new cheeses are coming on the scene to fill the gap. One of them is the strongly-flavoured Blue Shropshire which has a rich yellow paste and branching blue veins. This new cheese is being made by the Long Clawson dairy in Melton Mowbray, which was founded in 1911 as a co-operative to make Blue and White Stilton in the Royal Oak, a former village inn, and is still a farmer's co-operative covering four dairies.

This dairy company is in the forefront of the movement towards speciality cheeses – traditionally made, 'household name' cheeses with additional natural flavouring ingredients. In line with the current awareness of the fat content of foods, Long Clawson has produced a Cheddar cheese with half the regular fat content and a variety of flavours. In this range, besides the plain low-fat cheese, they produce ready-packed honey, cherry and almond, onion, chives and tarragon, and raisin and apple varieties.

In keeping with the geographical location, in the heart of 'pork pie country', the dairy has developed a range of Blue Stilton and pork pâtés with the addition of respectively, walnuts and celery, tarragon, and game, all made in what they describe as the traditional farmhouse manner, using no artificial flavouring or colouring.

Important though Derbyshire is in terms of dairying, it is no longer such a fruitful hunting ground for farmhouse cheese, and indeed the only such cheese production in the county is of Stilton, at the Nuttall's Dairy Crest dairy near Buxton. Confusingly, the only Derby cheese made according to the traditional method and recipe now comes from over the border, at Kirkby Malzeard in north Yorkshire.

Derby cheese is similar in texture to Cheddar, but more moist and with a more delicate flavour. The young cheese is mild in taste and honey coloured; as it matures it develops a fuller flavour and darkens considerably.

Sage Derby, the popular version of the cheese which contrasts visually so well with others on the cheeseboard, was originally produced in spring, to be ready at harvest festival time. Here was a hard, full-fat, bright green cheese made especially to celebrate the season of mellow fruitfulness in the dales.

Present-day Sage Derby is made by steeping sage leaves in chlorophyll which is blended with the curds after salting and milling. This gives the cheese the subtle flavour of the herb and an attractive, and also subtle, green marbled appearance.

If you want to buy a tasty cheese, do pay a visit to Fuller's dairy at Brickwall Farm. Long rows of cows in the milking parlour stare nonchalantly at visitors. You push through a heavy vertical curtain screen to go into the farm shop, and find yourself almost in the centre of the action. The cold counter is stocked with a range of soft cheeses, all additive free. Curd cheese, low in calories and fat, is a cultured skimmed milk set with rennet.

The latest newcomer to the Fuller's range is a Camembert-style soft cheese, which is ripened from within by injection with a white fungus, *Penicillium album*. This colourless mould works on the lactic acid present in the curd and eventually eliminates it. Once this first stage has been reached, a second fermentation sets in, which results in the destruction of the casein. By then, the cheese is ripe, beginning to soften and at its most enjoyable. To keep it that way, Jean Fuller, the cheesemaker, advises storing the cheese at a temperature of 4°C/38°F and allowing it to mellow at room temperature for a day before eating.

CHAPTER SIX

SPOILED FOR CHOICE
The Cheeses of the North of England

◆

To sit outside a country inn in rolling green pastureland, the sun glinting off the water as it scurries along a brook, a sparkling glass in one's hand and a plate of local cheeses on the table – that must come close to most people's idea of lunch-time heaven. And if that scene were set in the north of England, what would be the selection of farmhouse cheeses on offer? So many that the lucky diner would be spoiled for choice.

From Cheshire, a wedge of creamy-white hard pressed cheese that crumbles to the touch, and which a seventeenth century knight described as a 'quick, fat, rich, well tasted cheese', alongside its red, early-maturing counterpart, Red Cheshire, which remains refreshingly, crumblingly mild. And, richest of the county trio, the rare Blue Cheshire which is naturally mottled with dark veins and ripened over a longer period.

No North Country cheeseboard would be complete without a slice of young, immature, tingling White Lancashire, made traditionally from a mixture of two days' curd, with its piquant flavour and crumbly softness; so soft that the cheese can be spread easily with a knife. And Wensleydale, originally made with ewes' or goats' milk and now, produced from the milk of cows grazing the Yorkshire dales, just as creamy white, moist and fresh as it ever was. Such an embarrassment of riches, and that without any of the small-quantity, new, locally-made farmhouse cheeses that combine to make this region such a delight for the cheese gourmet.

The special qualities that we appreciate in true Cheshire cheeses have their origins deeply rooted in the past. In pre-historic times, the meadowlands of Cheshire and the surrounding counties formed part of the seabed and, now that they have been long-since reclaimed, still have rich underlying salt deposits. These, which farmers say contribute to some of the best grazing land in the country, progress through the complete dairying cycle, resulting in a high salt content in the milk and an ancient cheese variety with its unique, salty flavour.

The cheese was originally made throughout the Midlands and on the northwest lowlands, until Derbyshire and Leicestershire developed their own characteristic products. That left the home of Cheshire cheese largely where it is today, in dairies grouped around the south of Cheshire, the Vale of Clwyd, Shropshire and the north of Staffordshire. In the seventeenth century, dairyists from other regions, realizing that the secret of the cheese lay in the soil, tried to get in on the act and even carted some turfs away with them in an attempt to make 'real' Cheshire cheese! Unknowingly, however, they omitted to include the prime factor, the salt beds.

As befits its position as the oldest of all the traditional English cheeses, Cheshire long ago established a fine reputation. It is said – apocryphally – that the Romans built the wall around Chester, the capital of Cheshire, not so much to protect the city as its cheese industry; and the cheeses were sold in the *velabrium* or dairy market of ancient Rome. It was highly prized in London too and in the eighteenth century, Samuel Johnson and his literary friends were wont to while away the time in its namesake inn, Ye Olde Cheshire Cheese in London's Fleet Street, drinking ale and enjoying this versatile cheese. At that time there was another traditional, tea-time, accompaniment to the cheese – fruit cake.

This was the era when the cheese was enjoying its heyday and when in summer it was a case of 'all hands to the dairy' to help with the milking and cheesemaking. What were termed 'keeping cheeses' were pressed and matured for up to two years, a labour-intensive operation involving several changes of the cheesecloth binding, immersion in a brine bath and final salting. The cheeses were stored at unusually high temperatures, the ideal conditions found to be on a bed of hay under a thatched roof over the cowshed.

Because Cheshire cheeses were, and are, traditionally made from unpasteurized milk, there is no such thing as a cheese for all seasons. Those made in early spring, from milk with a higher acid content, are best enjoyed young and fresh; summer cheeses come into the category of 'medium keepers' while the autumn-made cheeses are the ones best left to mature fully, and will keep well for eighteen months or more. At least, they will if they are not waxed. It is a common practice now, condemned by some experts, to wax all Cheshire cheeses, with the consequent danger of sweating and detriment to long-term keeping.

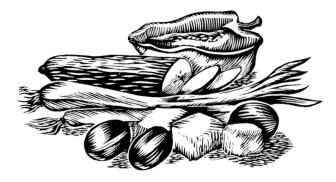

For the inside story of Cheshire cheesemaking, we turn first to Hawkstone Abbey Farm, a family-run business near Shrewsbury. Here Mrs Appleby has been making unpasteurized cheese from the farm herd of Friesians in the same time-honoured, time-taking way for over forty years. The secret of her White and Red Cheshires – and of the Double Gloucester cheeses she makes – is in the high degree of hand work involved, particularly in cutting the curd, which she does by hand to avoid damaging it.

After cutting, the curd is packed into moulds which are taken into the press room, where they are put into the original screw presses and come under pressure for two days. On the third day the cheeses are unmoulded, bound with cloth and simply 'put on the shelf to mature'.

Although production of the Appleby cheeses, in sizes from 1.25kg–22.5kg/2¾ lb–50 lb, is limited by the traditional methods of making them, they are distributed all over the country. Rosettes and certificates in the dairy bear witness to success at the top county shows, including Supreme Champion in two successive years at Nantwich, which for some time has annually held the biggest cheese show in western Europe.

'Blue Cheshire,' André Simon says in his 'Guide to Good Food and Wines', 'is not made – it just happens.' With a little help from specialists, that is to say. The leading specialist maker of Blue Cheshire – indeed the only farm solely devoted to making it now – is Hinton Bank Farm at Whitchurch, in Shropshire, where the Hutchinson Smiths run a Shorthorn/Holstein herd.

Group Captain Hutchinson Smith explains how it was, on his farm in days gone by, that this cheese 'just happened'. Every good Cheshire farmer in those days made cheese, especially in summer when there was a flush of milk from the rich pastures. The cheeses were left on the farm to ripen, some of them in cool dairies, until the autumn, when it was time to select the best for the great cheese fairs at Whitchurch, Nantwich and Chester. 'Very occasionally' a farmer would find one which was mottled throughout with a delicate blue mosaic – a complete mystery to everyone from the farmer's wife to the dairymaid.

What was known was that these cheeses were considered a great delicacy, and commanded a high price in the London shops. So the late Geoffrey Hutchinson developed his trade by buying in those he considered had the potential to 'blue', and matured them himself in the old beer cellars in Whitchurch.

It was not until a few years ago that Blue Cheshires began to be made specially at the farm on the Cheshire/Shropshire border, using fresh, unpasteurized milk from cows which graze the same rich pastures. Now, 'having unlocked the secret', they make hard pressed blue-vein cheeses weighing 9kg/20 lb, and 'Cryovac' halves.

This rich cheese, perhaps the strongest of all British cheeses, has a unique flavour which some people describe as bitter-sweet. The veining helps to break down the protein and fat, making the cheese more easily digestible.

The ideal temperature to store the Blue Cheshire is 9°C/48°F, and it should be closely covered with clingfilm or foil. Once frozen, it should be thawed in the refrigerator for two days. And to enjoy it to the full after dinner, experts recommend a glass of ruby port or medium or sweet Madeira.

We move northwards to Lancashire, where the cheese was first made by farmers in the Fylde, between the rivers Ribble and Lune which run through the county. This was originally a smallholder or smallfarm cheese, made in the kitchen from the product of two or three days' milkings, the curd cut by hand several times (which gives it the characteristic open, crumbly texture) and the cheeses ripened on shelves near the warmth of the kitchen range. Some cheese is still traditionally produced in the Lancashire hills, but the bulk of the production now takes place in creameries.

It was the growth of industry in its home county that brought Lancashire cheese both a wider audience and a more automated and speedy means of production. The cheese became the staple, nutritious food of mill workers in the burgeoning cotton towns, and in 1913 a creamery was opened in Chipping to cope with the increasing demand which farmhouses were unable to meet.

Much of the demand for Lancashire cheese has always been occasioned by its versatility in the kitchen. In everyday cooking, Lancashire cheese makes superb Welsh rarebit, fondue, sauces, toppings and soup. As an 'eating' cheese, it is especially good with fruity red wines or medium-dry sherry.

We call in at two farms in the Preston area which keep up the true tradition of Lancashire cheesemaking. At Lower Barker Farm, Inglewhite, Mrs Jean Butler uses 'all hand methods' to make the cheese from the unpasteurized milk of the Friesian herd which grazes from lush local pastures at the foot of Beacon Fell. She makes three sizes, 1.5kg, 9kg and 18kg/3 lb, 20 lb and 40 lb, of

Lancashire and Lancashire with sage cheeses which are sold from the farm and, through Mendip Foods, to major supermarkets.

At Beesley Farm, Goosnargh, Ruth Kirkham makes 20-kg/45-lb waxed Lancashire cheeses from the milk of the farm's Friesian herd. One of the problems in making cheese by the old method and without help, she says, is that it leaves her no time to welcome visitors to the farm. Mrs Kirkham's Lancashire cheeses are sold (in any cut weight) from the farm and nationwide under the Mendip Foods Farmhouse Cheese logo.

The traditional home of Wensleydale cheese, the dairy pride of Yorkshire, is the valley of the river Ure, which flows through the picturesque villages of Wensleydale and on through the widest and most densely afforested of the Yorkshire dales.

Tradition has it that the recipe for the cheese, then a closely-guarded monastic secret, was brought to Britain at the time of the Norman Conquest by the Cistercian monks who built Jervaulx and Fountains Abbeys, and handed down from one generation to the next. At that time, the cheese was made in the northern county entirely of ewes' and goats' milk (either or both) but gradually, and almost completely by the seventeenth century, cattle had usurped the small dairy animals.

The creamy-white cheese is made, mainly in the spring, autumn and winter months, from a finely-cut curd only lightly pressed. This leaves the flat-shaped cheese with a high moisture content, resulting in a light, slightly crumbly and flaky texture. The cheese is ripened for only about three weeks, and should be eaten young and fresh, when it is possible to appreciate fully its gentle, some say honeyed, after-taste.

Until World War II, when so much farmhouse cheese production stopped short never to start again, Blue Wensleydale was made in farms right along the valley and enjoyed a deservedly high reputation. This was principally a summer cheese, made from June to September in traditional cylinder shapes which 'blued' as they ripened. The cheese has – for it is still made on a limited scale – fine, lacy veins like a thin web breaking into the white paste, and a lighter, slightly more acid flavour than other British blue cheeses.

The Redesdale Wensleydale cheese follows a traditional recipe using a mixture of ewes' and cows' milk, both unpasteurized. The cloth-bound cheeses are matured for six to eight weeks and made in truckles of 500g–1kg/1 lb–2 lb and 3.5kg/8 lb.

From mid-May to December, Mark Robertson makes a natural mould-ripened semi-soft cheese in flat wheels from unpasteurized cows' milk. Coquetdale matures for five weeks, has a natural crust and weighs about 1.5kg/3 lb. No such seasonal restriction applies to North Tyndale, another semi-soft unpasteurized cows' milk cheese which is made all year round, matured for at least eight weeks, in 500-g, 2-kg and 8-kg/1-lb, 4-lb and 15-lb wheels.

Based on a Dutch Gouda recipe, Redesdale is an unpasteurized ewes' milk cheese, at least ten weeks old, with a washed rind, which is made in limited quantities all year round at its namesake dairy. Occasionally there are also fresh sheep cheeses with herbs, and Quark-style, low-fat cheese.

Stop for lunch at the village pub in Kirby Malzeard, near Ripon, and with the Dalesman's lunch you will be offered a delicious local cheese with a fine monastic pedigree. Coverdale, a white, crumbly cheese, is a local variation of one originally made from ewes' milk by the Cistercian and Benedictine monks in the great Yorkshire abbeys. The first recorded recipe for it dates from 1912, but by the early 1930s, in common with many other old Dales cheeses, it passed into local folklore and was no longer made. Now Les Lambert, the cheesemaker at Fountains Dairy, has revived this refreshingly mild local cheese which is made in 500-g, 1-kg, 2-kg and 5.5-kg/1-lb, 2-lb, 4-lb and 12–13-lb sizes.

Yorkshire is particularly well served by an Aladdin's cave of a specialist cheese shop, Mary's in Richmond, and a cheese wholesaler, Alan Porter (Provisions) who takes personal pride in the fine local produce of the region. Mary's shop in Trinity Church Square is a haven for cheese lovers, where Mr and Mrs Brian Richards have over eighty fine cheeses always in stock. Many of them have long local connections, and some recipes have been only recently revived by Yorkshire farmers and dairyists and are available in tantalizingly small quantities. With luck, you may find Alston, a tasty mixed cows' and goats' milk cheese; Tynedale and smoked Tynedale all from a Cumbrian farm; Botton, a hard, full-cream, unpasteurized Yorkshire cheese made to an old Dales recipe; Cotherstone, a dry-salted Wensleydale-style cheese; Allerdale, a Cumbrian goats' milk cheese; Ribblesdale and smoked Ribblesdale, both traditional goats' milk products, and Wensleydale, 'true Wensleydale,' Brian Richards says, 'more mature, and tastier than the traditional type, which we buy in small quantities from a number of local farms.'

CHAPTER SEVEN

A PERSONALITY ALL THEIR OWN
The Cheeses of Scotland

◆

Say Scotland. Say cheese. And almost inevitably one says 'Dunlop'. It makes for a more mouth-watering mind image, though, to continue the thought progression with the names of such delicious Scottish cheeses, some traditional, some new arrivals on the dairy scene, as Caboc, Crowdie, Bonchester and Dunsyre Blue, all proud products of the lowlands, highlands and islands.

Legend has it that the recipe for Dunlop cheese, which has been unkindly likened to 'soapy Cheddar', was brought from Ireland by a Protestant lady who had sought refuge from the religious up-heavals at the time of James II. She set up production in an Ayrshire dairy – calling the cheese first by that name – towards the end of the seventeenth century. This was the first whole-milk, semi-matured cheese to be made north of the border, and it must have been welcomed with open arms as a 'keeping cheese' – although it was always eaten relatively young – in the towns and cities. The more so because until then, the notoriously knife-resisting skimmed-milk Suffolk cheese had been off-loaded on to the Scots in huge quantities. And of this Southern cheese it was said, 'Hunger will break through stone walls and anything except a Suffolk cheese.' However, the Ayrshire cheese had its critics too, and one nineteenth-century commentator noted that it was 'not a very delicate cheese for the table'.

The Dunlop recipe, production methods and quality control came under southern scrutiny in the early nineteenth century, when a cheesemaker from the Cheddar region travelled to Scotland to take matters in hand, and some sixty years later, two Canadians introduced more mechanization and their own versions of Cheddar making. So it was, with this dual tutoring, that Scottish Cheddar was introduced, not really a contradiction in terms since the essential method was adhered to. The cheese was well matured, and was made alongside the mild, creamy and crumbly Dunlop on the farms.

'Those days have gone,' said a farmer-cheesemaker sadly, 'and farmhouse Dunlop and Cheddar with them. It's all made in the creameries now.' The details of mass-production take-over, milk quotas and unstoppable competition from the 'big boys' making block cheese has a familiar ring. But the good news is that a few 'real' farmhouse cheeses are made, for show-time, and do find their way into the shops. You just have to be in the right place at the right time to find them.

Perhaps there is cause for optimism that the tradition of Scotland's own hard pressed cheese will be revived, as some of the soft cheeses have been, so successfully, in recent years. One of these, now marketed under the brand name Highland Fine, is Crowdie, or *Gruth* in Gaelic, one of the oldest-known cheeses in the world, with a pedigree that predates the Viking invasion. It was once made on most of the crofts, but sadly fell by the wayside earlier this century. Crowdie, which is unique to the highlands and islands (the name derives from cruds, or curds) is a fresh, low-fat cheese, crumbly and with a subtle lemon flavour. It was the memory of eating this tasty cheese on oatcakes, and the old hand method with which his mother used to make it, that prompted highland farmer Reggie Stone, in 1962, to ask his wife, Susannah, to make some on their farm on the southern shores of Dornach Firth.

Susannah remembers how she heated a churn of fresh milk by standing it in a bath – the fireplace was not big enough – and constantly topping it up with hot water, and the next day straining the curd through a pillowcase. The result was a perfect cheese, but too much of it; they sent the surplus to the local shop, and a new era for the ancient cheese had begun.

The cheese is popular on at least two counts, with slimmers and with enthusiasts of another product of Scotland. Mrs Stone says that Crowdie comes into its own particularly before a ceilidh and at Hogmanay, as it is thought to limit the effects of prolonged whisky drinking!

A new version of the cheese, Black Crowdie, is a blend of Crowdie and fresh double cream, formed into oval shapes and covered with pinhead oatmeal and crushed peppercorns.

A cheese with an enthusiastic following south of the Border is Caboc, made to an ancient recipe handed down from mother to

daughter in Mrs Stone's family and which has been traced back at least as far as Mariota de Ile, the romantic daughter of the fifteenth-century Macdonald, Lord of the Isles. In those days it was the Chieftain's cheese, but now the farm cheesemaker Mrs Marsh, with Susannah Stone and her two sons, Jamie and Ruaraidh, make it for all of us to enjoy. The rich, double-cream cheese is rolled in toasted pinhead oatmeal and boxed in the Munro tartan of the Black Watch Regiment, which was raised by one of Reggie Stone's forbears.

Two new cheeses complete the Highland Fine range and, like the others, contain no rennet, artificial flavouring or colouring. Highland Soft (similar to the Lowland Ayrshire soft) which is a smooth, mild, full-fat cheese with a slightly sweet taste, and Galic. This is a natural soft cheese mixed with double cream, pepper and chopped fresh leaves of the locally-picked and, according to folklore, 'all healing' herb, wild garlic. The herb gives the cheese a light, bright flavour and leaves no after-taste. The cheese is rolled in crumbled and flaked toasted nuts and packed in heather-coloured Culloden boxes.

At Walltower Farm, Howgate, in Midlothian, Michael and Rosemary Marwick produce a whole Scottish cheeseboard of varieties, and offer to cater for any special orders, parties or gatherings. Among the Howgate specialities are yoghurt cheese; goats' milk cheese; cream cheese wrapped in oatmeal, or chopped nuts and bran, or black pepper; smoked soft cheese, and others resembling, respectively, Brie, Camembert and Gouda with a red wax covering.

Bonchester cheese has been making a name for itself all over Britain and, Scottish Borders farmer John Curtis tells us with justifiable pride, has twice been placed ahead of all French cheeses in its class at the prestigious Nantwich show. And what is its class? The cheese is a true 'fromage fermier' of the Coulommier type, made from the unpasteurized milk of John Curtis's Jersey herd – all eight of them. The cattle graze twenty-eight acres at Easter Weens, in the midst of the Cheviot Hills, are milked individually using a bucket and pipeline, and have a straw-bedded cubicle shed. Everything they need to produce the finest milk, in fact. 'After all,' the farmer concedes, 'they are the governors. We just do what they want.'

The evening's milk is chilled overnight and, as soon as the morning milking is over, is rewarmed and mixed with the fresh

milk. The cheeses are lightly salted. Animal rennet is used for the medium size and vegetarian rennet for the small ones. These and the starter culture are the only additives.

A food technology student lends a hand in the dairy during the long cheesemaking season, from mid March until the end of December. The maximum dairy capacity is 137 l./30 gal but at present John Curtis is happy to settle for a more manageable 113 l./25 gal, which produces thirty medium cheeses and sixty small ones. Even so, he is building a new dairy and cheese house to make a more compact unit.

With a distribution system of security vans calling twice a week, and the top London shops telephoning for repeat orders, it might be tempting to think that cheesemaking on this scale was an easy option. John Curtis hastens to disabuse anyone of that notion. It has taken him and his wife Christian seven years of getting up at first light and working for practically nothing to put Bonchester and Easter Weens on the map. And there is another contributory factor. He says that he is never entirely satisfied with either his cheese or his production methods – all his equipment comes from France – and is constantly seeking to improve both.

As to the product itself, Bonchester is a white-coated cheese which looks rather like Camembert and has a flavour somewhere between that of Camembert and Stilton, mild when it is young and strengthening considerably with age. Ripening starts on the surface and works inwards, the hard curd softening and changing to a deeper yellow colour with a stronger but more mellow flavour. Speed of ripening is entirely controlled by temperature and can

range from a day or two in a warm room to a month or more in the refrigerator. The cheese can be successfully frozen, but once thawed it will ripen and over-ripen more quickly than a fresh one.

Another success story, this one of a mould-ripened blue cheese, is told by Lanarkshire sheep farmer Humphrey Errington who has expanded his dairy production to include Dunsyre Blue, a cows' milk cheese. Having invested heavily in the buildings and equipment necessary to make his Lanark Blue ewes' milk cheese, it seemed a logical step to buy in Ayrshire milk and produce a sister cheese.

Strictly speaking, a cheese is only a 'country farmhouse cheese' if it is made from the milk of the herd or flock of the farm where it is made, but Humphrey Errington has no qualms about buying-in milk, and says he is lucky in the exceptionally high standards maintained at his neighbouring farm. The land is on the cold and windswept upland of the Dunsyre countryside, and the light loam soil is managed to give good swards of clover and timothy and other hardy grasses. 'The cows are content, they give good milk, good milk makes good cheese, and everyone's happy,' Mr Errington says.

The milk is collected every morning from Strathbogie Farm, Elsrickle, and taken in churns directly to the cheese vat at Ogscastle, where it is warmed and the process of fermentation begins. Samples of the milk are tested for cleanliness daily in the farm laboratory, and the strictest attention to hygiene is paid at every phase of production.

Dunsyre Blue, the only Scottish blue cows' milk cheese, is cured

for three months at 8°C/48°F in controlled high humidity. A constant low temperature is important in the home too – the cheese should be close-wrapped and kept at 3°–5°C/approx 38°F.

Looking back in sorrow, Humphrey Errington points out that fresh cream cheeses, hard cheeses and mould-ripened ones were regularly made on the farms as a means of using up the summer milk surplus. Now the torch is being carried by only a few Scottish farms. But with a growing market and increasing appreciation of 'real cheese', who knows? It could be the dawn of a new age.

CHAPTER EIGHT
FROM THE SHEEP AND THE GOATS
◆

'Ah,' said a man tasting the sliver of milky-white cheese offered to him in my local shop, 'that's a blissful September cheese, that is. Rich. Mild. And moist.' And suddenly he could see it all. The gentle, lettuce-green pastures speckled with woolly-ball shapes of contented sheep grazing their way ever closer to the milking shed, or the sharp, alert, perky little faces of a clutch of goats nuzzling their owner at a cottage door just down the road. 'Ah,' he said approvingly, 'I'll take a quarter of a pound of that one.'

And perhaps that little cameo, which came and went in a flash in the course of a morning's shopping, says it all. As a nation, we have a proud tradition of husbanding sheep and goats, one that long predates our recorded history. We love to see the animals out to pasture or mischievously tossing hay in a farmyard – it is a reassuring, comforting, friendly and incredibly therapeutic sight. And gradually we are re-acquiring a taste for the mild, lactic, sharp, brittle, nutty flavours of the ewes' and goats' milk cheeses that have been part of our dairying heritage for centuries. Though few of us, very few indeed, could boast a palate so refined that we could raise an approving eyebrow to the distinctive flavour of a 'blissful September cheese', or one made in July, for that matter.

And lastly, like the satisfied customer in a small East Anglian village store, when we do select these crumbly, tasty little cheeses, as yet we tend to buy them in small quantities. Which does not put sheep and goat keeping up there in the forefront of the moneymaking industries.

But, luckily for that discerning customer and all those of us who appreciate country cheeses, cash is not usually what the small dairy business is all about. Up and down the country, people who are making ewes' and goats' milk cheeses started just for the love of it, by keeping a few farmyard or backyard animals – many's the goat I have seen cheerfully tethered in the staight-up-and-down garden of a semi – and the milk, of course, just followed.

'What people who keep small dairy animals are doing,' says Mrs Olivia Mills, Honorary Secretary of the British Sheep Dairying Association, 'is keeping in touch with the soil. And when it comes to making cheese, the natural development of keeping sheep and goats, what we are selling to the public is romance.'

There *is* romance in these cheeses. In a truckle of soft Coulommier-type cheese produced from the milk of Friesland sheep and flavoured perhaps with herbs, chives or hazelnuts; in Sussex Slipcote, a full-fat soft cheese made, the farmer reminds us, from a recipe of Shakespeare's day; in Skirrid, a hard-pressed ewes' milk cheese marinated in mead, and in Beenleigh Blue, a full-fat, semi-hard cheese which comes from a Devon flock of Friesland/Dorset crosses.

There is romance, too, in the goats' milk cheeses made around the country, mostly from British Saanen and Toggenberg herds, such as the full-fat, hard Red Box goat cheese produced scientifically by a hobbyist in Suffolk; flat discs of golden-coated, rich, sweet Bozeat from Northamptonshire; Marianglas, a firm, cracked, buttery-yellow tome from Gwynedd, and Sattersleigh, a mild, solid little round cake of cheese with a mottled dusty-white and yellow coating from Umberleigh, in Devon.

It is only within the last decade that sheep and goat keeping has so captured the hearts and minds of smallholders. One reason – apart from the sheer delight of it – is that the milk of these small dairy animals enjoys the Ministry of Agriculture classification of 'food'. This means that it is not subject to the stringent regulations and milk-quota restrictions that beset the production of cows' milk. And that means that sheep and goat keepers can enjoy a greater degree of freedom. Not for them the see-saw situation of having to sell their milk production to the Milk Marketing Board and buy it back at a subsidized price, in order to turn it into a food. Their milk, from both sheep and goats, is a 'food' already!

Sheep Dairying

Traditionalists in this field have everything going for them. Sheep have been milked in Britain since time immemorial, and huge dairy flocks were kept until the late Middle Ages, when by far the highest proportion of all the cheese and butter produced was made of ewes' milk. Gradually over the centuries, and starting from the western regions, the dairy cow nudged the ewe from her position of prominence, until sheep dairying reached and long maintained an all-time low.

Now at last the clock is being turned back and a growing number of enthusiasts keeping one, two or a few ewes is recreating the traditional British ewes' milk cheeses that were made hundreds of years ago. Some British sheep dairyists are experimenting with close approximations of cheese types which are cast in familiar foreign moulds, and others are testing the market with new

texture and flavour combinations. All in all, it is good news for the cheese gourmet.

Think of sheep grazing and you think, quite rightly, of lush green pastures. This is more than a sentimental vision. It is the reality of sheep farming, since the quality of the ewes' milk and all the milk products will be in direct ratio to the nutritional value the animals derive from it. And so, to put the whole study of grass management in a nutshell, the better the grazing, the tastier the cheese. Any shortfall in the quality or quantity of the pasture can be offset to a degree with other crops, and a special feed is normally given to the ewes at milking time. But it is generally agreed that it is the nature of the grass and the minerals in the soil that affect the nature of the cheese.

Much is heard about grazing sheep on herbal pastures – fields and fields of wild thyme, camomile or marjoram drift into the mind's eye – in order to produce cheese that is flavoured at source, through the milk. But Olivia Mills maintains that whilst some herbs and vegetable crops may taint the milk, none enhances it. And she should know, since she lectures on cheesemaking and judges cheeses of all types at fairs and conventions all over the world. She cites kale as an example. Here is a lush, nutritious crop that imparts an unwelcome – some would say unpleasant – bitterness in the milk, and the only way to eradicate it is to pasteurize the milk and oxidize out the flavour. The only foodstuffs that improve the flavour of the milk, Mrs Mills emphasizes, are those that add to the fat content.

The flavour of sheep's milk cheeses has always been a matter of concern. Even in the Middle Ages, the natural taste derived from the milk and any maturing process was not always considered enough to make the cheese appealing. Some plain cheeses are frankly far too bland for many people's taste, and there is a growing public demand for what one producer refers to as 'cheese-withs' – cheese with onion, chives and other herbs, peppercorns, caraway or poppy seeds, garlic, walnuts, lemon, apricot, pineapple and others.

GOATS' MILK CHEESES

Everyone knows that goats are temperamental creatures, and the world's worst worriers – 'worse even than a poor old goat-keeper trying to scratch a living from his cheese,' as one East Anglian cheesemaker said mock-cynically. They, the goats that is, will go completely to pieces and the milk yield will suffer if their domestic arrangements are disturbed, the weather goes haywire or their feed is changed suddenly. Goats like a quiet life, and a nice steady routine. And they like to be petted, which is why 'keeping a few goats' proves such a therapeutic hobby to more and more people these days.

It is a fact that more goats are being milked in Britain now than has been the case for centuries – 'since time was' as an old farmhand put it. The most popular milking breeds are British Toggenburg, a soft creamy-brown colour with deep cream, friendly faces, British Alpine and British Saanen.

But unfortunately, not all of this rich, high-protein, 6 per cent fat content milk finds its way on to our cheeseboards or into our refrigerators. Many small producers simply turn the milk into curd, freeze the curd and sell it in bulk to a wholesaler. And off it goes to France, to be turned into delectable goats' milk cheeses which eager British gourmets bring back home as fine examples of what we in Britain should be producing. One of the problems is that whereas in France goats are traditional domestic animals, that is not, yet, the case on this side of the Channel. But we are working on it!

Even worse than the cross-Channel curd trade, from the point of view of the cheese gourmet, is the fact that many people who keep goats for show purposes do not sell the milk for cheese at all. They feed it to their, or somebody else's pigs.

Goats do not require a vast acreage, but in exchange for a high milk yield – which can continue for long periods even if they do not breed annually – they do like a high-quality feed. Grass alone is not enough because, unlike sheep, goats are not grazers. Browzers would be a better description of these munch-munch, sniffle-snaffle backyard animals. Hay, triticale and oats, a particularly high-fibre food, supplemented with natural feedstuffs such as steamed peas and sugar beet pulp suits them admirably.

The mountain-goat image of these tough little animals foraging about on steep gradients in all weathers can be somewhat misleading, and the domesticated British breeds are markedly less hardy. They need adequate shelter from the cold and rain and plenty of good, dry straw for bedding.

Unlike sheep and cows, and with the exception of large commercial herds, goats are not normally milked in a parlour. They are usually hand-milked into a bucket – bringing to mind images of a milkmaid sitting on a three-legged stool, her unruly hair kept in place by a frilly mob-cap – in a shed, or even in the open yard. This means of course, without going into the minutiae, that scrupulous hygiene is essential when handling the milk.

Once again the 'shall we, shan't we pasteurize, or freeze' milk argument rages thick and fast, and dairy goat-keepers are split on the relative merits as far as the end product, the cheese, is concerned. Most keepers insist that the best cheese is made with milk used immediately, straight from the udder so to speak, but this clearly imposes a strain on the cheesemaker, turning what may be a pleasant hobby into an inconvenient daily chore.

When milk has to be stored, to accumulate enough to make cheese in convenient batches, it can be quickly cooled and refrigerated at a temperature below 6°C/43°F, or successfully

frozen for up to three months. As with ewes' milk, the fat particles are very small and evenly distributed, and do not therefore inhibit freezing.

As for pasteurization of goat's milk, it is not necessary, from the pathogenic point of view, though some goat-keepers choose this as a means of short-term storage of the milk.

'Can it be successfully frozen?' one goat-keeper repeated. 'Not in my dairy, it can't,' and he went on to insist that 'the freezing process denatures the goats' milk far more than pasteurizing ever does.' What, then, is the would-be cheese gourmet to believe? The evidence of his own taste-buds as he samples one goats' cheese after another, clearly.

Perhaps it is in the sampling and enjoyment of goats' cheese more than any other factor that, as a nation, we in Britain could profitably educate our taste buds. In the past few years we have been buying more and more home-produced goats' cheese, but mostly at the milder end of the flavour scale. The strong billy-goat tang of some cheeses is definitely an acquired taste, but the whole spectrum of the cheeses should never be judged on a sample of one. Anyone who has only ever experienced one memorably 'goaty' cheese aromatically announcing its ripe old age is cordially invited to try, try, try again.

With soft goats' cheeses, the flavour advances considerably with age. The cheese usually takes three or four weeks to mature. As it ripens the liquid evaporates, the cheese becomes saltier, and hollows appear. (These are not faults, but entirely natural.) The rind yellows and, in some cheese types, becomes so pitted that it looks like the lunar surface – not a pretty sight. By week seven or eight, the flavour will have developed beyond recognition, and connoisseurs who thoroughly enjoy the cheese at four weeks may detest it a month later – or vice versa. A good retailer will have a note of the date when a farm-produced cheese was made, and customers should never be too timid to ask.

There is something of the thrill of a treasure hunt in seeking out new-to-you goats' cheeses. As one devotee puts it, 'Half the fun of sampling them is that you can't usually see the cheese for the wood – or the chestnut leaves, ashes, oatmeal, peppercorns or whatever. With all that exotic outer covering, no-one can possibly guess what the cheese inside is like.' But it is great fun trying!

CHAPTER NINE
CHEESEMAKING AT HOME
◆

A bath of water simmering on the stove and playing bain-marie to a bucket of fresh, steaming milk (the way to heat milk, even now); gleaming brass cooking pans and glinting brass cream skimmers on long, long handles; creamy stoneware bowls housing creamy setting curds; fine muslin tied at the top, utilitarian dolly bags straining more curds over a trough. Curd knives like giant combs with extra-long tines, and curd cutters like sturdy potato mashers with a single cross-bar; tin cheesemoulds with draining holes in decorative patterns, and stout wooden barrels with slats not quite meeting, for the same purpose; straw mats, round, oblong, oval, of every size and shape – what manner of cheeses have drained their whey through those basket weaves?

All this is sepia nostaglia, a vision – confined now to museums and a precious few survivalists – of cheesemaking, cottage style. A 'real' dairy would have added a curd mill, like a turn-handle mangle with a wooden chute, wood screw and spring-loaded presses and moulds of a size capable of holding half a hundred-weight of cheese. It was big business and hard work, especially in summer, keeping up with the yield from a milking herd or flock of sheep.

How does this backward glance relate to the way you can make cheese at home today? It shows that, unless you happen to own a milking herd, you can have the best of both worlds. Rejoice in continuing the link with the past, relax in the therapy of transforming one natural ingredient into another, yet make cheese (for your own home consumption) in a thoroughly modern kitchen as and when you feel like it. Making cheese for sale is a different matter and is subject to certain regulations – it should be made in a special cheese-room with 'hose-downable' walls, for one thing.

To make fresh and soft cheeses you do not need any specialist equipment. You can make a start the moment the mood takes you. In fact, kitchen or dairy hygiene at every stage of the process is infinitely more important than the paraphernalia involved. You can improvise cheese moulds from cake tins, yoghurt pots, new flower pots, bread baskets or bulb bowls, cut curds with the bread knife and press small cheeses between sheets of waxed paper in a flower press – but you cannot cheat on effective and safe hygiene.

In heating the milk to the right temperature (usually around blood heat) to encourage the growth of the organisms you want, you are creating perfect nursery conditions for other, harmful bacteria too. And so it is vitally important to sterilize every piece of equipment; the spoons you use for stirring and transferring the curds, the medicinal dropper for measuring the rennet, the moulds, the draining mats, everything, either by boiling them for five minutes or by immersing them in a sterilizing solution such as sodium metabisulphite. Take this as read in all the following recipes, 'Stand a sterilized colander over a sterilized bowl and line it with a double thickness of sterilized cheesecloth. . . . Tip the cheese into a sterilized bowl and stir in the salt with a sterilized spoon.' And so on.

On the subject of hygiene and the slaying of organisms, if you wish to pasteurize milk, the way to do it is this: heat it to exactly 85°C/185°F and cool it as quickly as possible, by standing the container in a large container of ice-cold water, to 21°C/70°F. If you are in any doubt about the standard of hygiene of the milk you use, you *must* pasteurize it. If you use frozen ewes' or goats' milk, sold in this form at many a cottage gate, thaw it in the refrigerator for twenty-four hours.

For all but the simplest types of cheese, it is advisable to use a starter culture of some kind. This culture, which contains a high proportion of *Bacillus lacticus,* lactic acid bacteria, encourages rapid growth of those bacteria present in the milk and at the same time, inhibits the growth of other undesirable enzymes. You can use buttermilk as a starter, many of the following recipes do. Make a 'purpose-built' one by soaking in warm milk a small piece of the cheese type you wish to make and then straining it, or buy a commercially prepared culture. These are available in many types, manufactured to give varying specific properties to the different types of cheeses.

Special cheese rennets (recommended for hard and semi-hard cheeses especially) are sold by the same suppliers (name and address on page 110). For other cheese types you can use rennet tablets or liquid rennet sold in chemists. If the instructions say 'dissolve the tablet in water', take it for granted that it means water you have boiled only moments ago, and instantly cooled.

Ewes' milk is particularly sensitive to the action of rennet and, as a rule of thumb, you need only one-fifth of the amount recommended for cows' and goats' milk cheeses. As a general guide (but follow specific recipes accurately) you need one drop of rennet per 1 l./1¾ pt milk for hard and semi-hard ewes' milk cheeses and two drops per 1 l./1¾ pt for fresh curd cheeses. Which means that the rennet content of the cheese will not break the budget – sixty drops makes just over half a teaspoon. When old shepherds ran out of the rennet they made from the extraction from young suckling lambs' abomasum (stomach), they turned instead, effectively, to a wild flower known as Cheese Rennet or Lady's Bedstraw (*Galium verum*) and stirred the warm fresh milk with bunches of that – sterilized, presumably.

Improvisation is the watchword of cheesemaking. If you do not have any rennet, use a bunch of herbs. If you do not have a gleaming stainless steel bucket to heat milk in a water-bath, use a plastic one that can be sterilized (never use galvanized iron). If you do not possess the 'correct' moulds (supplier's name on page 110), seek inspiration in the kitchen cupboard. Pierce holes in yoghurt pots for small, fresh cheeses. Pile curds into a loose-bottomed cake tin lined with cheesecloth for bigger cheeses, place a (sterilized) straw mat over the top and invert it. The whey drains through the straw and the cake-tin base (now on top of the curds) becomes a 'follower', a lid just made to slide down inside the mould as the curds compact and shrink under pressure. If you are impatient to make a cheese but do not have the suggested milk type, use what you have by adjusting the rennet proportions accordingly. Very little is lost if a small experimental quantity does not earn the accolade of the 'blissful September cheese' of the previous chapter. And a great deal is gained if it does.

'FRESH' CHEESES

BUTTERMILK CHEESE

Cultured buttermilk contains bacteria similar to those in cheese starter culture – and so it is, in effect, its own starter. The cheese is crumbly and slightly drier than cottage cheese, with a bright, sharp flavour.

◆

1 l./1¾ pt cultured buttermilk
1 teaspoon rock salt

◆

Slowly heat the buttermilk to 37°C/98°F, stirring once or twice. Remove from the heat, cover and set aside for 2 hours.

Stand a colander over a bowl and line it with a double thickness of scalded cheesecloth. Tip in the separated buttermilk, gather up and tie the corners of the muslin and hang it over the bowl. Leave it to drain for 2 hours.

Tip the cheese into a bowl and stir in the salt. Shape the cheese into a log or flat round and flavour with herbs or spices if you wish.

Makes about 350g/12 oz

LEMON CHEESE (ACID-CURD CHEESE)

Lemon juice provides the acid that helps to curdle the milk, and also adds flavour. The cheese is moist and spreadable and can be served plain, tossed with herbs or slightly sweetened.

◆

1 l./1¾ pt goats' or cows' milk
3 tablespoons lemon juice
1 teaspoon rock salt

◆

Slowly heat the milk to 37°C/98°F and pour it into a large bowl. Stir in the lemon juice, cover the bowl with cheesecloth and leave it in a warm place for 15 minutes, when the milk will have begun to set.

Stand a colander over a bowl, line it with a double thickness of scalded cheesecloth and gradually ladle in the curds.

Gather up the ends of the cheesecloth, tie them and hang over a bowl to drain for about 1 hour.

Tip the cheese into a bowl, stir in the salt and any other flavouring you wish.

The addition of finely-snipped chives and a few grindings of black pepper make a pleasant sandwich spread.

Makes about 300g/10 oz

YOGHURT CHEESE

If you make your own yoghurt – and which cheesemaker doesn't? – this is an economical cheese to make. It has a lovely fresh, light taste and a grainy texture.

◆

1 l./1¾ pt plain yoghurt
1 teaspoon rock salt

◆

Slowly heat the yoghurt until it separates.

Stand a colander over a bowl and line it with a double thickness of scalded cheesecloth. Tip in the curds, gather up the ends of the cloth and hang it over a bowl to drain for about 4 hours.

Tip the cheese into a bowl, stir in the salt and shape the cheese into rounds or logs.

Makes about 300g/10 oz

CREAM CHEESE

This is the one to serve with fresh or simmered fruits, to use for Coeur à la Crème, and to enjoy in rye-bread sandwiches. The cheese is smooth, rich and deliciously creamy.

◆

600ml/1 pt single cream
150ml/¼ pt double cream
3 tablespoons buttermilk
½ teaspoon rock salt

◆

Slowly heat the creams to 24°C/75°F. Stir in the buttermilk, tip into a bowl, cover and leave in a warm place for 8 hours.

Stand a colander over a bowl, line it with a double thickness of scalded cheesecloth and gradually ladle in the curds. Gather up the ends of the cheesecloth, tie them and hang over a bowl to drain for 2 hours.

Tip the cheese into a bowl, stir in the salt and the cream cheese will be ready. If you wish to make it into decorative shapes, turn it into moulds, cover and leave to drain for 1–2 hours.

Makes about 300g/10 oz

GOATS' MILK AND CREAM CHEESE

Make one successful batch of plain cheese and then let your imagination run riot. Rosemary or tarragon leaves, fennel or coriander seeds, oatmeal, herb-flavoured oil as a marinade – the sky's the limit for possible variations.

◆

1 l./1¾ pt goats' milk (or cows' milk)
600ml/1 pt double cream
3 tablespoons buttermilk
1 rennet tablet dissolved in water or ¼ teaspoon liquid rennet
1 teaspoon rock salt

◆

Slowly heat the milk, cream and buttermilk to 37°C/98°F. Remove from the heat and stir in the rennet. Set aside until the curds and whey have separated. Tip into a scalded colander and drain off the whey.

Cut the curd into 2.5-cm/1-in squares and place them in a cheese mould or tie them into a piece of scalded muslin and hang it to drain for several hours.

When the cheese is well drained, tip it from the mould or cloth into a bowl and stir in the salt. Shape the cheese into flat rounds, wrap it in clingfilm and store it in the refrigerator for 2–3 days.

Makes about 350g/12 oz

GARLIC AND PEPPER CURD CHEESES

The acid in the wine vinegar curdles the milk, and produces a soft, fresh cheese with large granules and a sharp, almost lemony flavour.

◆

4 l./7 pt milk
5 tablespoons white wine vinegar
3 garlic cloves, peeled and crushed
1 teaspoon salt
About 8 tablespoons crushed black peppercorns

◆

Gently heat the milk to simmering point, stirring occasionally. Remove from the heat, stir in the vinegar and continue stirring for 2 minutes. Set aside for 20 minutes.

Stand a colander over a bowl, line it with a double layer of scalded cheesecloth and gradually ladle in the curds. Gather up the corners of the cheesecloth, tie them with string and hang over a bowl to drain for about 2 hours.

Turn the curd into a bowl, mash it with a fork, stir in the crushed garlic and salt and mix well.

Divide the curd into 6 equal pieces and shape them into flat rounds. Toss the cheeses in the crushed peppercorns, pressing the spice on to cover the surface completely.

Place the cheeses on a board covered with greaseproof paper. Place another sheet and a board on top and leave under this light pressure for 24 hours.

Wrap each cheese in clingfilm and store in the refrigerator. The cheese will keep well for about 8 days.

Makes 6 x 50-g/2-oz cheeses

EWES' MILK CURD CHEESE

Every country that milks sheep has its own version of this mild, fresh cheese. The curds are soft and moist – in Holland it is known as 'wet cheese' – and take well to both sweet and savoury flavours.

◆

2.25 l./4 pt ewes' milk
5 drops rennet
2 tablespoons boiled water, cooled

◆

Slowly heat the milk to 32°C/90°F. Stir the rennet into the water and stir it into the milk. Continue agitating for 2 minutes, then cover and set aside in a warm room until the curds set.

Using a draining spoon, pack the curds into moulds with a pattern of holes. These can be heart-shaped coeur à la crème moulds, the traditional small wicker-work basket moulds or yoghurt pots pierced with holes. Stand the moulds on a tray, cover them with cheesecloth and leave to drain overnight.

The cheese should be stored in the refrigerator and eaten within a day. It is good as a dessert sprinkled with brown sugar, honey or a liqueur, and served with fruit, fruit purée or simply a topping of cream.

To make a savoury cheese, spoon the curds into a bowl and stir in salt before packing into the moulds, then pat chopped herbs or ground spices – paprika for example – on to the unmoulded cheese.

Makes about 500g/1 lb

RICOTTA-STYLE FRESH CHEESE

There is a limit to how much whey one can drink on a hot summer's day or use in scones, cakes and soups. Here is a way of using the protein that 'slipped through the net' when the curd was drained. The cheese is good in cheesecakes, salads and as a dessert.

◆

2.25 l./4 pt ewes' milk whey

◆

Bring the whey to the boil in a large pan and keep it boiling vigorously. Skim off the white froth that rises to the top – this constitutes the fatty acids left in the whey – and spoon it into moulds. Cover with a cheesecloth, leave to drain for 3–4 hours and use very fresh.

Makes about 250g/10 oz

WHEY CHEESE

Whey, the 'waste' product after draining the curds, is too good and too full of goodness to waste. This cheese is dry and crumbly and has a strong, sharp flavour. It is good in savoury pies, such as Greek cheese and spinach pies, and as a topping for green and tomato salads.

◆

4 l./7 pt whey

◆

Pour the whey into a large, heavy-based saucepan or preserving pan and bring it to the boil. Keep it at a gentle boil for about 3 hours, stirring occasionally. When most of the liquid has evaporated, and only the golden-coloured curds are left, lower the heat and stir the curd until it forms a thick, dry paste. (Take care that it does not 'catch' on the base of the pan.)

Remove the pan from the heat, turn the curd into a chilled bowl and stir for about 5 minutes, until it has cooled.

Spoon the curd into 2 small yoghurt pots or similar containers and level the tops. Cover with clingfilm or foil and place on a mat to drain for about 2 hours. Store in the refrigerator. The cheese will keep well for up to 2 weeks.

You can coat whey cheese in herbs, chopped nuts, spices or seeds – see the suggestions given for fresh cheese flavourings.

Makes 2 x 125-g/5-oz cheeses

VARIATIONS ON FRESH CHEESES

Variety is the spice of home-made fresh cheeses. The list of different variations is endless, so be a little adventurous! Here is a market-stall of ideas:

Stir into the drained curds:
a crushed garlic clove, or more to taste; any combination of fresh chopped herbs – make your own.

Fines Herbes Mixture:
finely-chopped fresh or canned pineapple or dried apricots; finely-chopped raw mushrooms, red, green, or yellow peppers; very, very sparingly, finely-chopped fresh red or green chillies (but never the seeds); sultanas, currants or chopped seedless raisins.

Roll the cheeses in:
finely-snipped chives or chopped fresh tarragon, marjoram, mint or other herb leaves; dried herbs such as oregano, thyme or summer savory, or a herb blend; paprika; crushed black or green peppercorns, allspice or juniper berries; fennel, caraway, coriander or cumin seeds; chopped walnuts, hazelnuts, almonds and others, or press on a few walnut or pecan halves; medium oatmeal; fine oatmeal mixed with ground ginger; dried grated orange or lemon peel.

Wrap the cheeses in:
fresh or dried bay leaves; chestnut or vine leaves.

Sandwich them between:
dried fennel stalks; thin strips of thinly-pared dried orange, lemon or grapefruit rind.

Garnish the cheeses with:
clusters of cinnamon, lemon, or orange-scented geranium leaves; sprigs of fresh or dried rosemary, summer savory or thyme.

GLISTENING IN OIL

One age-old way to keep fresh cheeses fresh and at the same time impart extra flavour is to store them in herb or spice-flavoured olive oil. Infuse sprigs of herbs – rosemary, bay leaves, what you will – or a spoonful of spice seeds in a jar of good-quality oil; cut the cheese into cubes or mini rounds, toss them, if you like, in crushed peppercorns and immerse them in the oil. Cover the jar and store it in a cool place.

Prepare jars of home-made cheese in advance, decorate with a ribbon and they make a fabulous gift!

SOFT CHEESES

COLWICK CHEESE

This soft cheese, which sets in a 'flan' shape with a hollow centre, is made to an old Scottish recipe. You can fill the hollow with fruit and cream – it is especially good with a mixture of soft fruits – or with, say, prawn and ham salad.

◆

4 l./7 pt milk
2 tablespoons buttermilk
24 drops cheese rennet
Rock salt

◆

Slowly heat the milk to 32°C/90°F and remove from the heat. Stir in the buttermilk and rennet and continue stirring for 2 minutes to distribute it evenly. Gently stir the top of the milk, to prevent the cream from rising (this was known as pushing down the cream) until the milk is thick enough to coat the back of the spoon. Tip into a large bowl, cover with scalded cheesecloth and leave at a warm room temperature for 2 hours.

Stand 2 moulds on a straw mat on a tray or draining board and line each mould with a double thickness of scalded cheesecloth. Carefully ladle the curds into the moulds. Allow them to drain for about 1 hour, and then cover the moulds by drawing the cheesecloth over the top.

Lift up the cheesecloth by gathering up the ends and gently 'bounce' the curds in the mould to facilitate draining. Leave the curds for 36–48 hours, lifting them up and 'bouncing' them occasionally, and replacing the mat with a fresh one once or twice.

Turn the cheeses out of the moulds and the cloths. Pat off the surface moisture with a pad of kitchen paper.

Sprinkle the surface of the cheese with salt, which will help to form a thin, dry crust and improve the keeping quality. Wrap in clingfilm and store in the refrigerator.

Makes 2 x 15-cm/6-in rounds

COULOMMIER CHEESE

This is the soft, full-fat cheese which, as we remark in the first chapter, is in almost every cheesemaker's repertoire these days. It can be eaten at three or four days old, or left to ripen for another week or more.

◆

2.25 l./4 pt cows' or goats' milk
¼ teaspoon cheese starter
¼ teaspoon cheese rennet
2 teaspoons boiled water, cooled
15g/½ oz rock salt

◆

Slowly heat cows' milk to 32°C/90°F, goats' milk to 29°C/85°F and stir in the cheese starter. Remove the container from the heat, cover it and leave in a warm place for 15–20 minutes.

Dilute the rennet in the water and stir it into the milk for 1 minute. Cover the container and leave it in a warm room (the warmth helps the satisfactory draining of the curds) for about 1 hour, until the curd has developed. Carefully strain the whey.

Place a cheese mould on a rush mat. (A special Coulommier mould is a 2-tier stainless steel cylinder which enables you to lift off the top half when the curd has sunk below that level.) Skim off the curd in slivers and lay them in the mould – the thinner the curds, the better they will drain – until the mould is full. Take care not to knock the mould, as it has no base the curd can easily slither away. Cover the mould with scalded cheesecloth.

As the curds settle in the mould, continue to fill it up until all the curd has been transferred.

Leave the mould undisturbed for about 12 hours. By then the curd will have settled enough for the top half of the mould – if you use a traditional Coulommier one – to be taken off. Reverse the curd in the mould on to a second (and of course sterilized) mat. Repeat this turning process twice a day for the next two days, turning the cheese five times in all, and then remove the mould.

Rub the cheese all over with the salt, wrap it in clingfilm and store it in a cool place.

This is a versatile cheese which takes well to the addition of chopped herbs, crushed garlic, spice and so on.

Makes 1 x 12.5-cm/5-in cheese

GOATS' MILK CHEESE

Wrap the cheeses in chestnut or vine leaves while they mature. The leaves protect the cheese, give a subtle flavour and look good on the cheeseboard.

◆

2 l./3½ pt unpasteurized goats' milk
2 tablespoons buttermilk
8 drops cheese rennet
About 20 sweet chestnut leaves or large vine leaves, washed and dried

◆

Slowly heat the milk to 32°C/90°F, remove from the heat and stir in the buttermilk and rennet. Continue stirring for 2 minutes, then cover with a cheesecloth. Leave in a warm room temperature for 2 hours, when the curd should be smooth, firm and rubbery.

Place 10-cm/4-in diameter moulds on a straw mat on a tray or draining board and ladle in the curds. Cover each mould with a scalded cheesecloth and place weights to fit inside the moulds. (If you use cleaned, used food cans for the moulds, use full cans of a smaller size for the weights, then stand something heavier on top.)

Leave the cheeses to drain for about 40 hours, putting a slightly heavier weight on top during the last day.

Turn the cheeses out of the moulds and pat the surface dry with a pad of kitchen paper. Make a ring of the leaves, stand a cheese in the centre and cover with another ring of leaves. Bring the top leaves down over the sides, bring the lower ones up and tie them around with fine string. Bind the string over and round, parcel fashion.

Leave the cheeses in the refrigerator for 2 days to ripen. Eat them within 8 days.

Makes 2 x 10-cm/4-in cheeses

SEMI-HARD CHEESE

SMALLHOLDER CHEESE

This is an example of a pressed cheese which gives satisfying results – it is mild and firm – in exchange for meticulous care and attention to detail.

4.5 l./8 pt cows' or goats' milk
2 tablespoons cheese starter
½ teaspoon cheese rennet
2 teaspoons boiled water, cooled
10g/⅓ oz rock salt
25g/1 oz lard, melted

Gently heat cows' milk to 32°C/90°F, goats' milk to 29°C/85°F and remove from the heat. Stir in the cheese starter, cover with a cheesecloth and set aside for 45 minutes.

Return the milk to the stated temperature. Stir the rennet into the boiled water, stir it into the milk and continue stirring for 2 minutes. Stir the top of the milk for at least 10 minutes, until it begins to set and resist the movement of the spoon. Cover, set aside in a warm room temperature for 45 minutes until the curd is firm.

Using a stainless steel knife with a long blade, cut the curd first in one direction and then the other until it is in very small pieces. Stir the curd and the whey thoroughly.

Slowly heat the whey by placing the container in a bath or large pan of hot water, stirring continuously until it reaches 38°C/100°F for cows' milk, 35°C/95°F for goats' milk. The curds should separate easily when pinched between thumb and first finger.

Cover a large container with a scalded cheesecloth and tie it firmly in place. Strain the curds and whey on to the cloth, untie it, gather up and tie the ends and hang it for about an hour for the curd to drain and settle.

Turn the curd into a bowl, break it into small pieces and stir in the salt.

Line a 12.5-cm/5-in mould with cheesecloth and stand it on a tray. Pack the curd into the mould, fit a lid inside the mould and put under 13-kg/28-lb pressure for about 8 hours. (Name and address of suppliers of cheese presses will be found on page 110.)

Turn the cheese out of the mould, turn it, wrap in a fresh, dry cloth and return to the mould. Increase the pressure to 18 kg/40 lb. On the following day, turn the cheese, replace the cloth, return to the mould and place under maximum pressure for a further 24 hours. Turn the cheese out of the mould. Melt the lard and brush it all over the cheese.

Cut three pieces of cheesecloth, two circles slightly larger than the diameter of the cheese and one exactly the depth of the cheese, and slightly longer than the circumference. Place one circle on the top and one on the bottom of the cheese and smooth the extra width over the sides. Wrap the long strip tightly around the cheese to 'bandage' the sides.

Leave the cheese in an airy place with a temperature of about 13°C/55°F to mature for at least 6 weeks, turning it daily for the first week, and then on alternate days.

Makes 1 x 12.5-cm/5-in cheese

SAGE 'FLET-MILK' CHEESE

An East Anglian skimmed-milk cheese adapted from a recipe in a Norfolk household book of the late eighteenth century. Of historical interest, there is also a version using Norfolk lavender flowers.

◆

4 l./7 pt skimmed milk
3 tablespoons buttermilk
15 drops cheese rennet
5 tablespoons single cream
2 handfuls of sage leaves, washed, dried and finely chopped
1 teaspoon rock salt
Fresh sage, to garnish

◆

Gently heat the skimmed milk to 35°C/95°F, then remove from the heat. Stir in the buttermilk and rennet and stir continuously for 2 minutes. Turn the milk into a bowl, cover with a cheesecloth and set aside at warm room temperature for 12 hours, when the curd should leave the sides of the bowl.

Cut the curd into 2.5-cm/1-in squares, stand the bowl over a pan of boiling water and heat the curd to 50°C/122°F, stirring frequently.

Place a colander over a bowl and line it with a double thickness of scalded cheesecloth. Tip in the curd, gather up and tie the ends of the cheesecloth and hang it over a bowl to drain for about 24 hours.

Tip the curd into a bowl and chop it finely. Stir in the cream, sage leaves and salt and spoon into a mould standing on a straw mat. Cover the mould with a lid which fits neatly inside (such as a plastic box lid with a slightly smaller circumference) and place a weight on top.

Leave the curd to drain under this pressure for about 20 hours.

Turn the cheese out of the mould, wrap it in waxed paper and put in the refrigerator for 24 hours to ripen. It will keep well for about 8 days.

Serve the cheese garnished with a sprig of fresh sage.

Makes about 400g/14 oz

FETA-STYLE CHEESE

The pure white, crumbly cheese is made in various parts of the world – Denmark, Greece, Cyprus and the Middle East. This recipe, from Mrs Olivia Mills, Hon. Secretary of the British Sheep Dairying Association, follows tradition and uses ewes' milk.

◆

2.25 l./4 pt fresh ewes' milk
8 tablespoons buttermilk
5 drops cheese rennet
2 tablespoons boiled water, cooled
Rock salt

◆

Slowly heat the milk to 68°C/155°F and keep it at that temperature for 30 seconds. Cool the milk to 28°–33°C/82°–92°F and stir in the buttermilk. At 32°C/90°F, stir in the rennet diluted in the water. Stir for 2 minutes, cover and leave in a warm room for 45 minutes to 1 hour to set.

Cut the curds into 2.5-cm/1-in cubes and keep the temperature of the curds and whey at a constant 32°C/90°F, until a small block of curd does not show a thumb mark when pressed. Scoop the curds into large moulds standing on a tray or draining board. Cover with cheesecloth and leave them to drain in a warm room for 2 hours.

Place a lid (follower) on the moulds and put on weights equal to the weight of the curds. Leave to drain for a further 4 hours.

Turn out the curd on to a board and break it up into flat blocks, like flaky pastry. Dip each piece into salt, pressing on as much as will cling to the curd. Stack the blocks on top of each other in an airtight container, fill it with fresh whey and seal the lid.

Set aside for 15 days, keeping the cheese at a temperature of 15-16°C/58-60°F. Then, depending on the type of container used, puncture or ease off the lid to release gas. Seal the container again and store it at 8°C/46°F.

To use the cheese, drain and dry it, wrap it in clingfilm and store in the refrigerator. Some people like to soak it in milk and water for a few days to get rid of the saltiness.

Makes about 500g/1 lb

SUPPLIERS OF
CHEESEMAKING EQUIPMENT

R & G Wheeler
Hoppings, Dunchideock, Exeter,
Devon EX2 9UL

Tel: Kennford 832238

Designers and makers of the Wheeler cheese press with small, medium or large moulds, drip tray and followers, and of – I think it is safe to say – everything needed for amateur and serious cheesemaking; cheese starter culture, rennet tablets and liquid rennet, dairy thermometer, ladles, cheese wax, butter muslin, and a complete Coulommier cheese kit including draining mats, boards and the distinctive two-tier stainless steel mould

Chr. Hansen's Laboratory Ltd.
476 Basingstoke Road, Reading RG2 0QL

Tel: 0734 861056

Suppliers to both trade and private customers of a very large range of specific cheese starter cultures, rennet powder and tablets, cheese colouring, cheese wax and general advice on dairying, including a booklet.

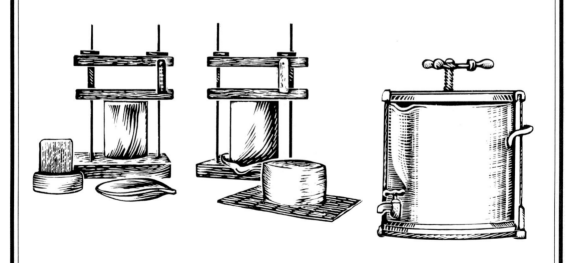

CHAPTER TEN
COOKING WITH CHEESE
◆

Creamy, full-fat fresh cheese that makes sweet and savoury cheesecakes so irresistible; tangy blue cheese in a glistening salad dressing; grated hard cheese stirred into a pastry mixture or sprinkled over a flan; wafer-thin slices of goats' milk cheese enfolded in chicken breasts – where would imaginative cuisine be if the cheese cupboard were bare?

The message is that cheese in cooking is infinitely versatile – mix and match many of the cheeses mentioned in the following recipes to discover just how versatile.

There is one golden rule, however: the harder, and more mature the cheese, the higher the temperature it can withstand. Spear a piece of well-ripened goats' milk cheese on the point of stick and hold it to the flames (as the Roman soldiers did, for a hot breakfast snack) and it will toast invitingly. Try the same trick with a ball of soft, fresh curd cheese and it will drizzle miserably away.

One more golden rule: never overcook or overheat cheese. The dreamiest, creamiest results may be achieved by stirring grated or diced cheese into hot sauces, soups or casseroles after they are removed from the heat. Cooking cheese in liquid is a recipe for disaster, a sure way to be faced with a cat's-cradle of chewy strings, high in protein and utterly lacking in eye and palate appeal.

Freezing Cheese

The answer to the alliterative question, 'Can you freeze cheese, please?' is yes, most definitely. Which is just as well, since we all get carried away at one time or another and buy far more than we can eat at the peak of perfection. All the hard and semi-hard cheeses, ripe, oozing soft creamy cheeses (Brie and Coulommier style) and cottage cheese take the cool temperature in their stride. The only exception is full-fat, fresh or cream cheese which emerges from cold storage dry, grainy and entirely devoid of that lively personality that made it so attractive in the first place.

Freeze cheese in portion sizes, that is to say in the quantities in which you can use it within a day or so of thawing. Close-wrap it in foil, seal it in a polythene bag, label it with the date and use it in rotation. Anything over about three months, and you are expecting too much of its good nature.

If you do freeze a large wedge of cheese, in anticipation of a party perhaps, thaw it slowly in the refrigerator.

Grated cheese is a splendid stand-by, an instant garnish for soups, topping for flans, a protein-boost for vegetable dishes and invaluable as a sandwich filling. Store grated cheese in a lidded box and use it by the handful, without thawing.

POTTED STILTON

An old Leicestershire recipe that ensures the cheese is enjoyable to the last crumb. Serve it as a first course with fingers of hot toast, or as a light lunch dish with tomato and basil salad.

◆

50g/2 oz softened butter
225g/7 oz Stilton cheese, without rind, crumbled
A pinch of gound mace
2 tablespoons port or brandy
3 tablespoons melted butter
12 walnut halves, to garnish
6 watercress sprigs, to garnish

◆

Beat the butter until it is creamy. Beat in the cheese and mace, using a blender or food processor if a very smooth paste is preferred. Beat in the port or brandy a little at a time.

Divide the mixture between six individual ramekin dishes and smooth the tops. Pour on the melted butter and tip the dishes to spread it evenly.

Cover the dishes with clingfilm and chill in the refrigerator, where it may be stored without spoiling for about 8 days.

Garnish each dish just before serving with the walnut halves and watercress.

Serves 6

MELT-IN-THE-MOUTH FRIED CHEESE

This has to be the most succulent first course ever!

◆

350g/12 oz full-fat soft cheese, such as Coulommier or Brie
Oil, for deep frying
1 lemon, cut into 6 wedges
6 parsley sprigs, to garnish
Batter
50g/2 oz flour
2 tablespoons olive oil
175ml/6 fl oz warm water
Salt
1 egg white

◆

To make the batter, mix the flour and oil to a thick paste. Gradually pour on the water, beating constantly, and season with salt. Cover and set aside for at least 2 hours.

Whisk the egg white until it is stiff. Beat the batter, and fold in the egg white.

Cut the cheese into even, bite-sized pieces.

Holding the cheese pieces on a fork or skewer, dip them into the batter.

Heat the oil in a deep pan and when it is hot, fry the cheese pieces, a few at a time, for 3 minutes. Remove them with a draining spoon and toss them on crumpled kitchen paper. Serve them at once, with the lemon wedges and parsley.

Serves 6

BLUE CHEESE IN A RING

Fill the centre of the ring with prawns, a chicory and pear salad, black grapes and orange segments, whatever – it makes a tasty first course or light lunch dish.

◆

2 tablespoons gelatine
4 tablespoons water
100g/4 oz blue ewes' milk cheese, without rind, mashed
2 eggs, separated
150ml/¼ pt double cream, beaten
100g/4 oz walnuts, chopped
3 tablespoons port
Lettuce leaves, to serve
Walnut halves, to garnish

◆

Dissolve the gelatine in the water and set aside to cool. Mix together the cheese, egg yolks and cream and stir in the walnuts, port and gelatine mixture. Whisk the egg whites until they are stiff, and fold them into the mixture.

Pour into a ring mould rinsed in cold water, cover and chill for about 2 hours to set.

Turn the mould out to a serving place covered with lettuce leaves and garnish it with the walnut halves. Fill the centre with whatever salad you choose.

Serves 6

TOMATO CHEESECAKE

◆

150g/6 oz digestive biscuits, crushed
75g/3 oz butter, melted
25g/1 oz Leicester cheese, without rind, grated

Filling
1 tablespoon gelatine
4 tablespoons orange juice
250g/8 oz full-fat fresh cheese
1 tablespoon tomato purée
250g/8 oz tomatoes, skinned, seeded and chopped
2 eggs, separated
3 spring onions, white part only, trimmed and finely chopped
2 tablespoons fresh chopped basil or
1 teaspoon dried oregano
1 teaspoon grated orange rind
Salt and freshly-ground black pepper
Basil or mint sprigs, to garnish

◆

Mix together the biscuit crumbs, butter and cheese and press them into a 20-cm/8-in flan ring on a baking sheet. Set aside to chill.

In a small bowl, sprinkle the gelatine over the orange juice and place in another bowl of hot water. Stir to dissolve.

Beat the cheese, tomato purée, chopped tomatoes, egg yolks, spring onion, chopped or dried herb and orange rind and season with salt and pepper. Pour on the dissolved gelatine and mix well.

Stiffly whisk the egg whites and fold them into the mixture. Pour over the prepared base, level the top and chill in the refrigerator for 2-3 hours, until the filling is set.

Remove the flan ring and garnish the top with herbs. Serve with a green salad and crusty bread.

Serves 6-8

GREEK CHEESE PIES

These are the *tiropitta,* take-away pies served warm at bakers throughout Greece – the Aegean equivalent of Cornish pasties.

◆

350g/12 oz Feta-style cheese
100g/4 oz curd cheese
1 egg, lightly beaten
2 tablespoons chopped parsley
A pinch of grated nutmeg
Freshly-ground black pepper
300g/10 oz filo pastry
50g/2 oz butter, melted
water, for sprinkling

◆

Mash the cheeses and beat in the egg and parsley. Season the mixture with nutmeg and pepper.

Slice through the sheets of filo pastry to cut them in half across the width.

Working quickly and brushing each sheet of pastry lightly with melted butter, build up layers of the paper-thin paste. Cover the 'pastry in waiting' with a damp teatowel to prevent it from drying out.

Make three layers of the pastry squares and spoon filling well apart on two adjacent sides – for example, the centre top and centre right. Fold over the pastry to make a triangle enclosing the filling and cut the triangles in half. Continue with the remaining pastry and cheese filling.

Place the cheese triangles on a greased baking sheet, brush the tops with butter and sprinkle lightly with water. Bake them in a moderately hot oven, 190°C/375°F/Gas Mark 5 for 40-45 minutes, until the pastry is crisp and golden brown. Serve warm.

Makes about 12 pies

BELVOIR GOURGÈRE

◆

300ml/½ pt milk
75g/3 oz butter, diced
Salt and freshly-ground black pepper
100g/4 oz flour, sifted
4 eggs
100g/4 oz Stilton cheese, without rind, chopped

Salad
2 dessert apples, cored and diced
2 sticks tender celery, thinly sliced
4 spring onions, trimmed and sliced
50g/2 oz walnut halves
4 tablespoons soured cream
2 teaspoons olive oil
2 teaspoons lemon juice

◆

Line a baking sheet with non-stick silicone paper.

Put the milk and butter into a saucepan and bring to the boil. Remove the pan from the heat, season with salt and pepper and stir to blend the ingredients. Tip in the flour all at once, beating vigorously until the mixture is glossy and leaves the sides of the pan. Add the eggs, one at a time, beating until the mixture is smooth before adding the next. Stir in the cheese.

Spoon the mixture to make a large ring. Bake in the centre of a moderately hot oven, 190°C/375°C/Gas Mark 5 for 35–40 minutes, until the ring is well risen and golden brown.

Serves 4-6

TUNA AND PRAWN QUICHE

◆

250g/8 oz wholewheat flour
Salt
100g/4 oz butter
50g/2 oz Cheshire cheese, without rind, grated
About 3 tablespoons water, to mix

Filling
198g/7 oz can tuna in brine, drained and flaked
250g/8 oz Cheshire cheese, without rind, grated
100g/4 oz shelled prawns
1 green pepper, seeded, cored and finely chopped
2 eggs, beaten
3 tablespoons milk
150ml/¼ pt single cream
Salt and freshly-ground black pepper
A pinch of cayenne
2 tomatoes, sliced

◆

To make the cheese pastry, sift the flour and salt into a bowl and tip in any bran remaining in the sieve. Rub in the butter and stir in the cheese. Sprinkle on the water and mix to a soft dough. Wrap the dough in clingfilm and chill in the refrigerator for at least 30 minutes.

Roll out the dough on a lightly-floured board and use it to line a 23-cm/9-inch flan dish. Fill the flan case with the tuna, cheese, prawns and green pepper. Beat the eggs, milk and cream, season with salt, pepper and cayenne and pour the mixture into the flan. Arrange the tomato slices in a pattern on top.

Bake the flan in a moderately hot oven, 200°C/400°F/Gas Mark 6 for 40 minutes, protecting the pastry rim with a ring of foil if necessary. Serve hot, with a chilled green salad.

Serves 6

ASPARAGUS MERINGUE FLAN

◆

25g/1 oz butter
2 tablespoons flour
300ml/½ pt milk
100g/4 oz Wensleydale cheese, without rind, crumbled
2 egg yolks
Salt and freshly-ground black pepper
350g/12 oz asparagus spears, cooked (or canned ones, drained)
1 x 18-cm/7-in shortcrust pastry case, baked

Topping
2 egg whites
Salt
50g/2 oz Wensleydale cheese, without rind, grated
Paprika

◆

Melt the butter in a small saucepan, stir in the flour and gradually pour on the milk, stirring constantly. Simmer over low heat for 3 minutes, then remove from the heat. Stir in the cheese and egg yolks, season with salt and pepper and beat well. Set aside to cool.

Arrange the asparagus spears in a wheel pattern in the pastry case, reserving 2 or 3 tips for garnish. Pour the sauce over.

To make the topping, whisk the egg whites with a pinch of salt until they are stiff, and fold in the cheese. Spread the meringue over the flan case.

Bake in a moderate oven, 180°C/350°F/Gas Mark 4 for 15–20 minutes, until the meringue is set and golden brown. Allow to cool. Sprinkle with paprika and garnish with the reserved asparagus tips. Serve with a tangy green salad.

Serves 4–6

LAKELAND LOAF

◆

500g/1 lb wholewheat self-raising flour
1 teaspoon salt
1 teaspoon mustard powder
25g/1 oz butter
2 sticks tender celery, finely chopped
100g/4 oz Cheshire cheese, without rind, grated
1 egg
About 150ml/¼ pt milk
1 egg, beaten, to glaze

◆

Grease a 1-kg/2-lb loaf tin.

Sift the flour, salt and mustard powder into a bowl and tip in any bran remaining in the sieve. Rub in the butter and stir in the celery and cheese. Beat the egg with half the milk and add it to the dry ingredients, beating all the time. Pour on enough of the remaining milk to make a kneadable dough. Knead the dough on a lightly-floured board until it is pliable and free of cracks.

Press the dough into the prepared tin and brush the top with beaten egg.

Preheat the oven to 190°C/375°F/Gas Mark 5 and bake for 45–55 minutes, until the loaf is well risen and golden brown and sounds hollow when the tin is tapped underneath.

Leave to cool slightly in the tin before turning out. Serve warm or cold, spread with curd cheese. The bread is also delicious with butter and honey.

Makes 1 x 1-kg/2-lb loaf

FARMHOUSE SCONE RING

Coils of cheese and herb scones served warm with a colourful spread – delicious morning or tea-time snack.

◆

250g/8 oz self-raising flour
Salt
50g/2 oz butter
1 teaspoon dried oregano
150ml/¼ pt milk
125g/5 oz Lancashire cheese, without rind, grated
1 teaspoon celery seeds

The Spread
75g/3 oz cream cheese
2 tablespoons soured cream
2 tablespoons chopped parsley
50g/2 oz honey-baked ham, without fat, finely chopped
Freshly-ground black pepper

◆

Sift the flour and salt, rub in the butter and stir in the dried herb. Pour on the milk to make a firm dough. Knead the dough lightly until it is free of cracks.

Lightly flour a pastry board and roll out the dough to a rectangle about 23 x 33cm/9 x 13 in. Sprinkle 100g/4 oz of the cheese over the scone dough, and roll it up from one of the short ends. Cut the dough into eight slices.

Arrange the coiled dough pieces flat on a baking sheet in a circle so that they just touch each other. Sprinkle them with the remaining cheese and the celery seeds.

Bake the scones in a hot oven, 220°C/425°F/Gas Mark 7 for 15-20 minutes, until they are well risen and golden brown.

Makes 8 scones

APRICOT AND RAISIN CHEESECAKE

◆

50g/2 oz softened butter
50g/2 oz caster sugar
1 egg
50g/2 oz self-raising flour
½ teaspoon baking powder
1 teaspoon grated orange rind

Filling
350g/12 oz curd cheese
150ml/¼ pt double cream
25g/1 oz desiccated coconut
25g/1 oz plain flour
50g/2 oz caster sugar
3 eggs, beaten
75g/3 oz dried apricots, finely chopped
50g/2 oz seedless raisins
1 tablespoon sifted icing sugar
2 tablespoons apricot jam, sieved
75g/3 oz ground hazelnuts
4 thin slices orange

◆

Grease and line an 18-cm/7-in square cake tin.

To make the spongecake, mix together all the ingredients – it's a quick-mix recipe – and beat until the mixture is smooth. Pour into the prepared tin and bake in a moderate oven, 160°C/325°F/Gas Mark 3 for 15 minutes, until it is firm to the touch.

To make the filling, mix together the curd cheese, cream, coconut, flour, caster sugar, eggs, apricots and raisins. Pour the filling over the spongecake base and level the top.

Bake in the oven for 1¼ hours, turn off the heat and leave the cake for 30 minutes.

Turn the cheesecake out of the tin and brush the sides with apricot jam. Press on the ground hazelnuts to cover the sides completely.

Decorate the top with the orange slices.

Serves 8

CONGLETON APPLE PIE

◆

250g/8 oz wholewheat flour
½ teaspoon ground cinnamon
1 tablespoon caster sugar
100g/4 oz margarine
1 egg yolk
About 2 tablespoons water

Filling
1 teaspoon ground cinnamon
2 tablespoons soft light brown sugar
2 tablespoons flour
350g/12 oz cooking apples, skinned, cored and diced
5 tablespoons single cream
100g/4 oz Cheshire cheese, without rind, grated

◆

To make the pastry, sift the flour, cinnamon and caster sugar into a bowl and tip in any bran remaining in the sieve. Rub in the margarine and stir in the egg yolk. Sprinkle on the water and mix to make a stiff dough. Knead the dough lightly, wrap it in clingfilm and chill in the refrigerator for about 30 minutes.

Roll out two-thirds of the pastry and use it to line a 20-cm/8-in flan ring on a baking sheet. Mix together the cinnamon, brown sugar and flour, sprinkle the mixture over the pastry base and arrange the apple slices on top in rings. Pour on the cream.

Roll out the remaining pastry and cut it into 6-mm/¼-in wide strips. Arrange them in a lattice pattern over the flan, dampening and trimming the edges.

Bake the flan in a hot oven, 220°C/425°F/Gas Mark 7 for 25 minutes. Sprinkle on the cheese and return to the oven for a few minutes until it has melted. Serve warm.

Serves 6–8

CRÈME FRAÎCHE

The slightly tangy flavour of the French Crème Fraîche, which is fermented and thickened cream, is especially good contrasted with, for example, the sweetness of poached dried fruits and meringues. It makes a luxury instant topping for creamy soups, steamed vegetables and pasta dishes.

◆

600ml/1 pt double cream
300ml/½ pt soured cream

◆

Mix the creams together, cover the bowl with cheesecloth and leave at room temperature for about 6 hours, until the cream has thickened.

Stir the cream and store it in a lidded container in the refrigerator for up to eight days.

A different version, which borrows the cultured starter of buttermilk to start ripening the cream, is made by stirring 3 tablespoons buttermilk into 600ml/1 pt double cream.

Makes 900ml/1½ pt

CURDS AND WHEY

Junket is a traditional farmhouse dessert which used to be made in the milking parlour, using warm milk straight from the cow. It is through this simple yet delicious dairy dish that many cooks are first introduced to using rennet.

◆

600ml/1 pt full-cream milk (gold-top is best)
1 tablespoon caster sugar
1 junket tablet, crushed, or 1 teaspoon liquid rennet

◆

Slowly heat the milk to 37°C/98°F and remove from the heat. Stir in the junket or rennet and pour the milk into a serving dish.

Leave it at room temperature without disturbing it – if you move the dish, the curds will separate – for about 2 hours, until it is set.

Plain junket is a delicious accompaniment to summer fruits or, with its yoghurt-like consistency, is a dessert in its own right. You can give it a subtle flavour by stirring in 1–2 tablespoons rosewater or orange-flower water, and a luxury touch by very carefully spooning double cream over the top. A scattering of scented damask rose petals was considered the ultimate in elegance in Georgian times.

Serves 4

COEUR À LA CRÈME

No wonder it is colloquially called 'la crème de la crème', this deliciously light yet rich accompaniment to summer fruits. The dessert is traditionally prepared in heart-shaped moulds.

◆

250g/8 oz full-fat cream cheese
2 tablespoons sifted icing sugar
¼ teaspoon vanilla essence
150ml/¼ pt soured cream or double cream

◆

Line 4 heart-shaped coeur à la crème moulds with a double layer of scalded cheesecloth; or shape hearts from heavy-duty foil, or line decorative biscuit cutters with foil and pierce holes in the base.

Beat the cheese until it is light and fluffy, stir in the sugar and vanilla essence and beat again. Lightly stir in the soured cream or double cream.

Spoon the mixture into the lined moulds, piling it up into a mound. Fold the ends of the cheesecloth over to cover, and stand the moulds on a deep plate. Place them in the refrigerator overnight.

Turn out the drained and chilled moulds on to serving plates.

Flatter the creamy hearts with the best fruits summer has to offer – strawberries, raspberries, loganberries, blueberries, very lightly-poached blackcurrants, whatever.

Serves 4

SPICY WALNUT SABLES

Crisp and crunchy snack biscuits to serve with drinks.

◆

75g/3 oz flour
Salt
¼ teaspoon cayenne pepper
75g/3 oz butter
75g/3 oz mature Cheddar cheese, without rind, grated
Flour, for dusting
1 egg, beaten
6 tablespoons chopped walnuts
Rock salt

◆

Sift the flour, salt and cayenne and rub in the butter. Stir in the cheese and form the mixture into a smooth paste.

Lightly dust a pastry board with flour, roll out the paste and cut it into 2 x 5-cm/2-in strips. Brush with beaten egg and sprinkle with the walnuts and a little rock salt. Cut each strip into triangles and place them on a baking sheet.

Preheat the oven to 190°C/375°F/Gas Mark 5 and bake the pastries for 10 minutes, until they are golden brown. Transfer them to a wire rack to cool, and store them in an airtight tin.

Makes about 24

CHEESE 'TRUFFLES'

Unusual snacks for a drinks party.

◆

250g/8 oz full-fat fresh cheese
100g/4 oz blue cheese, without rind, crumbled
2 tablespoons Dijon mustard
Freshly-ground black pepper
5 slices pumpernickel bread, finely crumbled

◆

Beat together the cheeses and mustard and season the mixture with pepper. Scoop out teaspoons of the mixture and roll each one into a ball. Roll them in the pumpernickel crumbs to coat them completely. Chill.

Spear the 'truffles' with cocktail sticks to serve.

Makes about 24

SELECTED CHEESEMAKERS
COWS' MILK CHEESE

Berkshire

Cheesemaker: Mrs Anne Wigmore
Village Maid, Spencers Wood, Reading, Berks Tel: 0734 884564
Not open to visitors.
Cheeses: 'Wellington' Golden Guernsey cheese – a new British
cheese produced by Village Maid at their Spencers Wood dairy, on
the edge of the Duke of Wellington's estate. The cheese is matured
in the cellars of Stratfield Saye House, Basingstoke. A full-fat hard
cheese, made from unpasteurized milk, with no colouring or other
additives.
Where to buy: James's, Beckenham High Street, Kent; County
Delicacies, St Mary's Butts, Reading; The Mousetrap, Peascod
Street, Windsor, Berks; Wells' Stores, Streatley, Berks.

Cardiganshire

Cheesemakers: Welsh Organic Foods Ltd, Lampeter,
Cardiganshire
No visitors.
Cheese: 'Pencarreg', a new organic Welsh cheese, made from
organically produced unpasteurized milk from four family-run
farms in Cardiganshire. This is a full-fat soft cheese with a smooth
creamy texture, and containing only vegetarian rennet.
Where to buy: Alan Porter (Provisions) Ltd, Roecliffe,
Boroughbridge, N Yorks and other speciality suppliers.

Cheshire

Farmers: Richard and Tina Barnett
Cheesemaker: Paul Fowles
Henry Barnett & Sons, Overton Hall, Malpas, Cheshire SY14
7DG. Tel: 0948 860519

How to get there: Off the A41 at Hampton roundabout, to Malpas village, and ¾ mile left on Tilston road. Guided tours around the cheese factory, parties of 12 or more by appointment.
Cheeses: Traditional unpasteurized Farmhouse Cheshire in both white and red types. Made in 1-kg/2-lb, 9-kg/20-lb and 23-kg/50-lb sizes, but can be bought in any amount. Also iced Jersey cream.
Where to buy: From the Hall's Farm Shop; Owen, Owen Food Hall, Chester and other good cheese shops.

Derbyshire

Creamery Manager: R A Davies
J M Nutall & Co,
(Dairy Crest Foods), Dove Dairy, Hartington, Buxton, Derbyshire
SK17 0AH. Tel: 0298 84496
No visitors.
Cheeses: 'Dairy Crest' Stilton cheese, traditionally made and winner of Stilton Class at major cheese shows.
Where to buy: Most retail outlets.

Devon

Farmer: J G Quicke & Partners
Manager: Tom Langdon-Davies
Cheesemaker: Barry Rowe
Woodley, Newton St Cyres, Exeter, Devon EX5 5BT Tel: 039 285 222
How to get there: Situated 3 miles W of Exeter on the A377, beyond Newton St Cyres village.
Cheeses: Traditional farmhouse Cheddar in 25-kg/56-lb cylinders in mature, mellow and vegetarian mild qualities; Double Gloucester in 16-kg/35-lb size; Single Gloucester in 14-kg/30-lb size – all in quarters and smaller cuts.
Where to buy: From the Farm shop; 'all good delicatessens'; Paxton & Whitfield, Jermyn Street, London; Marks & Spencer (Traditional Cheddar).

Farmer: A N & L A Dickman
Cheesemaker: Ann Dickman
Wheatland Cheese, Winkleigh, Devon EX19 8DJ Tel: 083 783 361
How to get there: Wheatland Cheese is 1½ miles NE of Winkleigh.

Signed off the B3220. School parties welcome in the afternoons.
Cheeses: 'Wheatland Cheese' – an unpasteurized full-fat soft
cheese with a white crust, in 200-g/8-oz sizes, with only salt and a
vegetarian coagulant added. 'Wheatland Moor', an unpasteurized,
semi-hard cheese in 750-g, 1.5-kg and 2.5-kg/1½-lb, 3-lb and 5-lb
rounds.
Where to buy: At the farm or good delicatessens and cheese shops,
both locally and elsewhere.

Dorset

Farmer: Streatfield Hood & Co Ltd
Managers: Philip Crawford, Amanda Streatfield
Cheesemaker: Ken Corben
Denhay Farm, Bridport, Dorset DT6 5NP Tel: 0308 22770
How to get there: Take B3162 out of Bridport, turn left to
Broadoak, second turning left in village. (Farm shop open Mondays
and Thursdays, 9.30 am – 5.00 pm.)
Cheeses: Denhay Cheddar – traditional farmhouse Cheddar in 2-
kg/4½-lb cartonned 'Dorset Drums' and also 25-kg/56-lb cylinders.
(Any size cut from farm shop.) Cheeses are matured for up to one
year.
Where to buy: Direct from the farm shop (see above), or range of
stockists in Dorset, Somerset and Hampshire; Dorset Drums,
Selfridges, London; Hampers, East Molesey, Surrey; featured by
Waitrose Supermarkets.

Farmer: Dorset Blue Cheese Company
Cheesemaker: Mike Davies
Woodbridge Farm, Stock Garland, Sturminster Newton, Dorset
Tel: 0963 23216
How to get there: No sales from farm.
Cheeses: Now the only maker of Dorset Blue Vinney cheese in
Britain. Made in the traditional manner from unpasteurized milk
from their Friesian herd. Available for the Christmas trade in 1.5-
kg–2.5-kg/3½-lb–5½-lb truckles, otherwise in 6.5-kg–7.25-kg/14-
lb–16-lb drums.
Where to buy: Selected delicatessens on the south coast, Dorset,
Somerset and Yorkshire; Harrods and Selfridges, London;
James's, High Street, Beckenham, Kent; Wells' Stores, Streatley,
Berks.

Essex

Farmer: Robert Fuller
Cheesemakers: Jean Fuller
Fullers Ltd, Brickwall Farm, Sible Hedingham, Halstead, Essex
CO9 3RH Tel: 0787 60329
How to get there: In village, on A604 Halstead to Haverhill Road.
Cheeses: Low-fat curd cheese. Medium-fat soft cheese, from
pasteurized Jersey milk, both mixed with herbs and garlic or rolled
in fresh herbs. Cottage cheese.
Where to buy: From the farm shop, in shops in the Halstead,
Braintree, Dunmow, Colchester, Ipswich and Cambridge area. The
Honey Pot, Woodford Green, Essex; Bosworths and Natural Foods,
both Loughton, Essex.

Gloucestershire

Farmer and Cheesemaker: Charles Martell
Laurel Farm, Dymock, Glos Tel: 053 185 637
Not open to visitors.
Cheeses: Single Gloucester, sometimes with nettles and herbs, in
4-kg/8-lb rounds. Double Gloucester, usually uncoloured in 4-kg/
8-lb rounds. Double Berkeley, in 4-kg/8-lb rounds.
Where to buy: From the farm and markets in Cirencester,
Gloucester and Ledbury.

Hampshire

Farmer: Duke of Wellington
Cheesemaker: Mrs Anne Wigmore
Stratfield Saye, Basingstoke, Hants
Not open to visitors.
Cheeses: 'Wellington' Golden Guernsey, unpasteurized waxed and
natural rind, 2.5-kg and 5-kg/5-lb and 10-lb sizes. Soft Coulommier-
type pasteurized cheeses with garlic and herbs or chives from
Friesian cows' milk, in 250-g/8-oz rounds. Lactic curd cheese, same
flavours, in 100-g/4-oz pots.
Where to buy:
Wellington cheese: James's, High Street, Beckenham, Kent;
County Delicacies, St. Mary's Butts, Reading, Berks; Wells Stores,
Streatley, Berks; The Mousetrap, Peascod Street, Windsor, Berks.
Soft cheese: Locally, in farm shops.

Lanarkshire

Farmer: Humphrey Errington
Manager: Humphrey Errington
Cheesemaker: Ian McClhery
H J Errington & Co, Walston Braehead, Ogscastle, Carnwath,
Lanarkshire Tel: 089 981 257
How to get there: Visits by appointment. ½ mile N of A721, on the
Walston Road.
Cheeses: Mould-ripened Dunsyre Blue, from the unpasteurized
milk from Ayrshire cows. Scotland's 'only blue cows' cheese', it is
cured for three months in conditions of stable temperature and
high humidity. Also made Lanark Blue ewes' milk.
Where to buy: Good cheese shops and delicatessens nationally and
W M Low supermarkets.

Lancashire

Farmer: T & J M Butler
Cheesemaker: Mrs J M Butler
Lower Barker Farm, Inglewhite, Preston, Lancs PR3 2LH Tel:
0995 40334
How to get there: 4 miles on Beacon Fell Road, from Junction 32 of
M6. By appointment.
Cheeses: One of the few farms producing the original crumbly
Lancashire Farmhouse, using traditional methods. Sizes made
range from 1.5-kg/3-lb miniatures to 9-kg/20-lb and 18-kg/40-lb
cylinders. Also made from their Friesian herd is the lesser known
Lancashire Sage. Farm butter is also available.
Where to buy: Farm Dairy, Longridge, Preston; Mendip Foods,
Whitchurch, Salop; Neal's Yard Dairy, Covent Garden, London
WC2; supermarkets including Sainsburys, Tesco, Asda and
Morrison.

Farmer/Manager: John Kirkham
Cheesemaker: Ruth Kirkham
Beesley Farm, Mill Lane, Goosnargh, Preston, Lancs PR3 2FL Tel:
Broughton 865335
No visitors.
Cheese: Traditional farmhouse Lancashire, made in 20-kg/45-lb
waxed cylinders.

Where to buy: Direct from Beesley Farm; Mendip Foods, Mendip, Salop.

Leicestershire

Farmer: Webster's Dairy Ltd
Cheesemaker: M Fropwell
Saxelbye, Melton Mowbray, Leicestershire Tel: 0664 812223
How to get there: Visits by appointment only.
Cheeses: Webster's Blue Stilton and White Stilton, made by traditional hand methods, at the smallest Blue Stilton dairy, established in Saxelby for over 100 years.
Where to buy: From Webster's Dairy, 3.5-kg/8–8½-lb half Stiltons, or by mail order for whole 7.5-kg/16–17-lb Stiltons, and selected delicatessens, and large food stores, such as Fortnum & Mason, Piccadilly, London.

Company: Tuxford & Tebbutt
Manager: A M Farquharson
Cheesemaker: Howard Lucas
Thorpe End, Melton Mowbray, Leicestershire LE13 1RE. Tel: 0664 500555
No visitors.
Cheeses: Traditional Blue Stilton in 7-kg/16-lb sizes. Also Red Leicester cheese.
Where to buy: Most supermarkets and specialist shops, both in the region and elsewhere.

Midlothian

Farmer/Manager: Michael Marwick
Cheesemaker: Rosemary Marwick
Walltower Farm, Howgate, Penicuik, Midlothian Tel: Penicuik 72263
No visitors.
Cheeses: Cream cheese, wrapped in oatmeal or nuts and bran, or black pepper; lactic curd cheese; Gouda-type in red wax; Camembert and Brie types; smoked soft and 'Howgate' yoghurt cheese and some goats' cheese.
Where to buy: Shops in Penicuik, Peebles and Edinburgh, Scottish Cheese Board, and special orders by arrangement.

Northumberland

Farmer/Cheesemaker: Mark Robertson
Redesdale Dairy, Soppitt Farm, Otterburn, Northumberland
NE19 1AF Tel: 0830 20506
How to get there: 1½ miles off A696 on B6341, and signposted
'Cheese Farm'. Open daily (see below).
Cheeses: Real Wensleydale, from mixed Ayrshire cows' and ewes'
milk, unpasteurized and matured for 6–8 weeks. Available in
cloth-bound truckles of 500g and 3.5kg/1 lb and 7½ lb. North
Tyndale, an unpasteurized cows' milk cheese, semi-soft and
matured for a minimum of 8 weeks, in 500-g, 2-kg, 8-kg/1-lb, 4½-lb,
and 8-lb wheels. Coquetdale, a semi-soft, natural mould-ripened
cheese in flat wheels with natural crust, in 1.5-kg/3¼-lb weight.
Also made, Redesdale sheeps' cheese. Quarg-type cheese,
cheesecakes and yoghurt. Honey, jams and other farm produce.
Where to buy: From Redesdale Dairy (coffee, Shepherd's lunch and
teas available, picnic area, sheep milking demonstrations).
Cheeses from Corbridge Larder, Corbridge, Starker & Letham,
Hexham, both Northumberland; Partners, Barnard Castle; Neal's
Yard Dairy, Covent Garden, London WC2; The Real Cheese Shop,
High Street, Wimbledon, London SW19; Wells' Stores, Streatley,
Berks. Wholesale – Alan Porter (Provisions) Ltd, Roecliffe,
Boroughbridge, N Yorks.

North Yorkshire

Speciality Cheese Suppliers: Alan Porter (Provisions) Ltd
Bar Lane, Roecliffe, Boroughbridge, North Yorks Tel. 0432 322323
Cheeses: Suppliers of a wide range of cheeses from the dales of
Yorkshire and other 'speciality cheeses' from the north country
and elsewhere. Two goats' cheeses are Ribblesdale in 1-kg/2-lb–
2½-lb sizes, a smoked variety and Beasdale, made in the north
Yorkshire dales, distinctive with its coating of red wax.
Where to buy: Specialist shops nationally and some supermarkets.

Nottinghamshire

Company: The Colston Bassett & District Dairy Ltd
Manager and Cheesemaker: E T Wagstaff
Colston Bassett, Nottingham NG12 3FM Tel: 0949 81322
No visitors.

Cheeses: Mature Stilton cheeses in a range of sizes. One of only two 'farmhouse' makers, and the only one making unpasteurized Stiltons.
Where to buy: Selected retail outlets and specialist cheese shops, both locally and elsewhere.

Pembrokeshire

Farmers: Leon and Joan Downey
Cheesemaker: Leon Downey
Llangloffan Farm, Castle Morris, Near Mathry, Haverfordwest, Pembrokeshire SA62 5ET Tel: 0345 241
How to get there: Take A40 out of Haverfordwest to Fishguard. Turn left at Letterson crossroad (B4331). At Castle Morris turn right. (Farm is open most weekday mornings to view the cheesemaking.)
Cheeses: Llangloffan unpasteurized full-fat hard cheese with natural crust, made from the milk of Jersey cows. Available in 1.5-kg, 4-kg, 9-kg and 14-kg/3-lb, 9-lb, 20-lb and 30-lb sizes. Also made is Red Llangloffan, with chives and garlic, in 1.5-kg and 4-kg/3-lb and 9-lb rounds.
Where to buy: Direct from farm shop and by mail order. Specialist cheese shops such as Neal's Yard Dairy, Covent Garden, London, WC2, and Wells' Stores, Streatley, Berks.

Ross and Cromarty

Farmer: Mrs E R Stone
Manager: James Stone
Cheesemaker: Mrs Marsh,
Highfield Fine Cheeses Ltd, Blarliath, Tain, Ross & Cromarty
How to get there: North end of Tain, down Shore Road, first right and straight on.
Cheeses: 'Highland Fine', a soft, fresh traditional Scottish highland and island cottage-style cheese (Crowdie); and also Caboc cream cheeses, rolled in toasted oatmeal, and Galic, a full-fat soft cheese, mixed with local wild garlic leaf, double cream and pepper. Available in 100-g/4-oz tartan packs and 900-g/2-lb oblongs.
Where to buy: From the dairy as above; North of Scotland Milk Marketing Board, Claymore House, Ardconnel Terrace, Inverness; Crowson & Sons Ltd, 17–23 Farringdon Street, London EC1, and other wholesalers.

Roxburghshire

Farmer: Mr & Mrs J R Curtis
Manager and Cheesemaker: Miss Marjory Young
Easter Weens, Bonchester Bridge, Near Hawick, Roxburghshire
TD9 8JQ Tel: 045 086 635
How to get there: Parties by prior arrangement only.
Cheeses: Prize-winning Bonchester cheese, of the Coulommier
type – with a flavour 'between Camembert and Stilton'. Made from
the unpasteurized milk of Jersey herd, with white crust, maturing
to a strong flavour. In sizes 100g/4 oz, 280g/10 oz and 2kg/4 lb.
Cream and yoghurt sold from the farm only. (Holiday chalets
rented.)
Where to buy: Commercial orders, direct from farm; Simpson
Foods, Bonnington Road Lane, Edinburgh; Ivor Leighton, 2 Gately
Walk, Stockton-on-Tees, Cleveland; Alan Porter (Provisions) Ltd,
Bar Lane, Roecliffe, Boroughbridge, N Yorks; J & P Langman,
Perrots Brook Farm, Cirencester, Glos; Harvey & Brockless, 44
Stewarts Road, London, SW8; James's, 188 High Street,
Beckenham, Kent; and other national stockists.

Shropshire

Farmer: Appleby's of Hawkstone
Cheesemaker: Mrs C A Appleby
Hawkstone Abbey Farm, Weston-under-Redcastle, Shrewsbury,
Shropshire Tel: 0948 840387
No visitors.
Cheeses: Prize-winning White and Red Appleby's Hawkstone
Cheshire cheeses, hard pressed, calico cloth-bound, and made in
1.5-kg/2¾-lb, 3-kg/7-lb, 7.5-kg/17-lb, and 22.5-kg/50-lb cylinders.
Double Gloucester, cloth bound, in 2-kg/4-lb, 7-kg/15-lb and 14-kg/
30-lb 'cylindricals'. Also sold, hard pressed unpasteurized goats'
milk cheese, cloth bound in 3-kg/7-lb and 4.5-kg/10-lb cylinders.
Where to buy: Specialist cheese shops, delicatessens; Paxton &
Whitfield, Harrods and Neal's Yard Dairy, all London; Wells'
Stores, Streatley, Berks.

Farmer: Hutchinson Smith & Son
Cheesemaker: Miss R M Harrison BEM
Hinton Bank Farm, Whitchurch, Shropshire SY13 4HB Tel: 0948
2631

How to get there: By appointment only. One mile N of Whitchurch on A49.

Cheeses: Sole makers of hard pressed Blue Vein Cheshire, made from unpasteurized milk from their Shorthorn/Holstein herd. Available in whole cheeses, 9-kg/20-lb and Cryovac halves, 4.5-kg/ 10-lb sizes.

Where to buy: Mollington Farmhouse Cheese Ltd, Mollington Grange, Chester; Mendip Foods, Whitchurch; and most cheese factors.

Somerset

Farmer: John Green
Cheesemaker: David Higdon
Newtown Farm, West Pennard, Glastonbury, Somerset BA6 8NN
Tel: 0458 32952
How to get there: Approx 3 miles from Glastonbury, and 6 miles from Shepton Mallet on the A361.
Cheeses: Traditional hard pressed Cheddar, from Friesian herd.
Where to buy: The Truckle of Cheese, Glastonbury; Cheese Board, Wells; some supermarkets in London and the south east.

Farmer: Viscount Chewton
Manager: Mrs Marian Shaw (Cheese Sales)
Cheesemaker: Peppy D'Ouidio
Priory Farm, Chewton Mendip, Somerset BA3 4NT Tel: 076 121 666
How to get there: On the A39, 6 miles NE of Wells and S of Midsomer Norton.
Cheeses: Traditional farmhouse Cheddar from pasteurized milk, bound in cheesecloth and available in 2-kg, 3-kg and 4-kg/1-lb, 6-lb and 9-lb truckles, as well as 25-kg/56-lb cylinders.
Where to buy: From the farm shop at Chewton Cheese Dairy, where the restaurant serves home-cooked lunches.

EWES' MILK CHEESE

Cornwall

Farmer: Geoffrey Bersey
Cheesemaker: Jill Isaac
Sheviock Barton, Sheviock, Torpoint, Cornwall PL11 3EH Tel: 0503 30909
How to get there: Visits by appointment only. Situated opposite church in village of Sheviock.
Cheeses: Soft unpasteurized cheese like Brie in appearance, average weight, 1kg/ 2 lb. Full-fat, unpasteurized semi-hard, plain or cider flavoured, approx. 2kg/ 4 lb.
Where to buy: From farm. Otherwise mainly sold in London.

Dumfriesshire

Farmer: Michael Neilson
Cheesemaker: Carol Neilson
Windyknowe, Annan, Dumfriesshire DG12 5LN Tel: 04612 4691
How to get there: Situated ½ mile off B722 Annan–Eaglesfield Road, towards Brydekirk.
Cheeses: Barac hard cheese, matured for a minimum of three months. Unpasteurized, natural rind and original, in 1.5-kg/3-lb size. Also Baby Barac, approximately 600g/1¼ lb. Soft cheese to order in summer.
Where to buy: About thirty specialist cheese shops throughout the UK. Also wholesale and retail direct from farm.

Dyfed

Farmer: Don Ross
Cheesemaker: Karen Ross
Mesen Fach Farm, Bethania, Near Llanon, Dyfed SY23 5NL Tel: 097 423 348
How to get there: Coast road Aberath–Cardigan. B4577 to Tregaron, through Pennant, Cross Inn, Bethania, past Dalgetty sign on right, turn right down to crossroads, right again (phone box on right) and take right at fork, then ½ mile on left is Mesen Fach.
Cheeses: 'Acorn' hard full-fat sheeps' cheese, natural rind, unpasteurized milk.

Where to buy: 2-kg/4–4½-lb truckles from leading cheese factors, specialist outlets or direct by mail order.

Hampshire

Farmer/Cheesemaker: Mrs Olivia Mills
Wield Wood Estate, Alresford, Hants SO24 9RU Tel: 0420 63151
How to get there: 2 miles SE of Preston Candover, just outside Upper Wield.
Cheeses: 'Walda', a Gouda-type sheep cheese either plain or with added green peppercorns in 1-kg/2-lb and 2-kg/4-lb sizes. Unpasteurized, waxed rind. Also sells sheep milk.
Where to buy: Locally – Foodsmiths, Basingstoke; Alresford Delicatessen; Secretts Farm Shop, Milford, Surrey; Lidgates, Holland Park Road, London; and most wholefood shops.

Shropshire

Farmer: John E Dakin
Cheesemaker: Elizabeth Dakin
Wackley Farm, Burlton, Shrewsbury, Shropshire SY4 5TD Tel: 093 922 660
How to get there: 10 miles NW of Shrewsbury on the A528.
Cheeses: Soft Coulommier-type cheese made from 100 per cent unpasteurized ewes' milk and sea salt. Available in 500-g and 2-kg/ 1-lb and 4-lb sizes. Ewes' milk sold.
Where to buy: 'Any good cheese shop'.

Somerset

Farmer: E P White
Cheesemaker: N Gregory
Willett Farm, Lydeard St Lawrence, Taunton, Somerset Tel: 09847 328
How to get there: Visits by appointment. 5 miles from Bishops Lydeard (A358), on B road to Raleigh's Cross and Lydeard St Lawrence.
Cheeses: 'Colesford Blue', a full-fat mild blue cheese, made from unpasteurized ewes' milk.
Where to buy: Some London cheese shops and delicatessens and local shops in the Taunton area.

Suffolk

Farmer/Cheesemaker: Mrs Ann James
Ostler Dairy Flock, Horringer, Suffolk Tel: 0284 88281
How to get there: Visits by appointment. A143 2 miles S of Bury St
Edmunds, adjacent to National Trust Ickworth Park.
Cheeses: 275-g and 350-g/10-oz and 12-oz rounds, also soft cheeses,
chive flavour and others.
Where to buy: Direct from farm shop.

Sussex

Farmer: Mark Hardy
Cheesemakers: Mark Hardy, Katherine Mowbray
Putlands Farm, Duddleswell, Uckfield, East Sussex TN22 3BJ Tel:
0825 712647
How to get there: On the B2026, between Fairwarp and
Duddleswell.
Cheeses: Halloumi cheese (a traditional Cyprus cheese), Feta from
100 per cent ewes' milk, Sussex Slipcote, a full-fat soft cheese,
plain or with herbs and garlic, Ricotta, a low-fat soft cheese,
'Duddleswell' hard ewes' milk cheese, mature 2-kg/4-lb cheeses.
Also sheeps' milk.
Where to buy: From the farm; throughout the south east and
London and parts of the north. Good delicatessens; wholefood and
cheese shops.

GOATS' MILK CHEESE

Devon

Cheesemaker: Robin Congdon
Ticklemore Cheese Shop, Ticklemore Street, Totnes, Devon TQ9
5EJ Tel: 0803 865926
How to get there: Visits by arrangement. Cheese Shop is at the
bottom of Fore Street, Totnes, down an alleyway.
Cheeses: Ticklemore Fresh Goat Cheese – Coulommier-type, 75-g/
3-oz rounds (only from shop). Ticklemore Blue – a full-fat hard
goats' milk cheese in 1.5-kg–2-kg/3-lb–4-lb sizes, a firm, smooth
pressed cheese. Harbourne Blue, a full-fat goats' milk cheese in
2.5-kg–3-kg/5-lb–6-lb sizes. Rich, creamy, piquant blue-veined

cheese. Also available, Beenleigh Blue – a full-fat ewes' milk cheese, fairly strong, blue-veined, semi-hard cheese, available Sept–March. Also a range of British farmhouse cheeses.
Where to buy: Ticklemore Cheese Shop, Totnes; James's, High Street, Beckenham; Neal's Yard Dairy, Covent Garden, London; Wells' Stores, Streatley, Berks; and other specialist cheese shops.

Gwynedd

Smallholder/Cheesemaker: Mrs Jean Rickford
Maes Mawr, Llanllyfni, Caernarfon, Gwynedd LL54 6DG Tel: 0286 881809
How to get there: 7 miles S of Caernarfon on A487. Along Lon Ty Gwyn Lane by chapel, past school and over fields.
Cheeses: 'Marianglas' matured, pressed smallholder cheese with natural crust, 500g/1 lb, made from unpasteurized milk. Also soft cheeses blended with chives and rolled in paprika, in 100-g–500-g/ ¼-lb–1-lb rounds and whole milk soft cheese, blended with mixed dried fruit and rolled in black pepper. Also fresh and frozen milk.
Where to buy: Direct from house, local shops and Wells' Stores, Streatley, Berks.

Sussex

Farmers/Cheesemakers: Mr & Mrs W B Thomson
Holt Valley Farm, Underhill Lane, Clayton, Near Hassocks, Sussex Tel: 07918 5158
How to get there: One mile S of Hassocks and Hurstpierpoint.
Cheeses: Small, fresh herb cheeses, about 100-g/4-oz each, to order. Fresh, pressed mature cheese with hard crust (like Feta). Also frozen goats' milk.
Where to buy: The Delicatessen and Nature's Corner, both Hassocks; The Brighton Cheese Shop, Kensington Gardens, Brighton; The Home Delicatessen, George Street, Brighton; Frances Minny, Hurstpierpoint; Jacksons Delicatessen, Rock Street, Kemptown, Brighton; The Gourmet Delicatessen, Seven Dials, Brighton.

INDEX

Cheese names only are
included

A

Allerdale 74
Alston 74

B

Beenleigh Blue 85
blue cheeses 17–18, 33–5,
    54–5, 60–4, 65, 68, 70–2,
    73, 81–2, 113, 115, 118, 129
Blue Shropshire 65
Blue Vinney 17, 35, 54–5
Bonchester 78–81
Botton 74
Bozeat 85
Brie 16, 35
buttermilk cheese 94–5

C

Caboc 15, 77–8
Caerphilly 32, 56
Camembert 16, 35
Cheddar 28, 30, 32, 40–8, 65,
    76, 128
Cheshire 17, 33, 68–72, 119,
    121, 125
    Blue 17, 35, 68, 70–72
Colwick 102
Coquetdale 74
Cotherstone 74
Coulommier 16, 35, 56, 78,
    104–5, 114
Coverdale 74
cream cheese 15, 78, 96–7,
    126, 127
Crowdie 15, 77
curd cheese 15, 25–6, 35, 56,
    66, 98, 99

D

Derby 32–3, 66
    Sage 33, 66
Dunlop 76
Dunsyre Blue 81–2

E

ewes' milk cheeses 35, 56, 73,
    74, 84–8, 93, 99, 100, 115

F

Feta 16, 109, 117

G

Galic 78
Gloucester, Double & Single
    32, 47, 48–53
goats' milk cheeses 35, 73, 74,
    84–5, 88–9, 97, 105–6

H

Highland Fine 77–8

I

Ilchester 47–8

L

Lancashire 33, 68, 72–3, 122
lemon cheese 95
Llangloffan 57–8

M

Marianglas 85

P

Pencarreg 58

Q

Quark 15

R

Red Box Goats' Cheese 85
Red Leicester 32, 64–5
Redesdale 74
Ribblesdale 74
Ricotta 15
Roquefort 17, 35, 50

S

sage cheese 33, 66, 108
Sattersleigh 85
Skirrid 85
Spenwood 56
Stilton, Blue 17, 35, 60–4, 65,
113, 118
    White 28, 32, 64
Sussex Slipcote 84–5

T

Tynedale 74

W

Wellington Golden
    Guernsey 56
Wensleydale 33, 68, 73–4, 120
    Blue 35, 73
Wheatland 56
whey cheese 100–1

Y

yoghurt cheese 96